Adulthood is an accessible text which deals with the vital area of adult psychological development in a concise and friendly form. The book's approach encourages engagement with the main theories and evidence of this highly relevant topic, as well as including less well-known models of adulthood for discussion.

The book begins with a definition of lifespan psychology, and further chapters include early and middle adulthood; the life events approach; marriage; parenting; divorce; and old age. It includes some modern slants on the classic research, as well as the up-to-date theories, and alternative theories are introduced. Cross-cultural issues and examples have been included in every chapter, and various biases are identified and explained. The final section has sample essays on this topic with extremely helpful examiner's comments, as well as a useful glossary.

Evie Bentley has written an ideal guide to this topic, which requires little or no background knowledge. It provides a useful introduction for both A-level and undergraduate students of psychology or sociology, and will also be of interest to anyone in the health or social care professions and to those with a general interest in developmental psychology.

Evie Bentley is Head of Psychology at Hillview School for Girls and at Hugh Christie Technology College, Tonbridge, Kent. She is also an Adult Education Psychology Tutor, West Sussex (Burgess Hill and Crawley), and Tutor and Second Year Module Leader in Developmental Psychology for International Correspondence Schools on line Psychology degree.

Routledge Modular Psychology

Series editors: Cara Flanagan is a freelance academic author and an experienced teacher and examiner for AS and A2 level psychology. Philip Banyard is Associate Senior Lecturer in Psychology at Nottingham Trent University and has 20 years experience as a Chief Examiner for GCSE and A level Psychology.

The *Routledge Modular Psychology* series is a completely new approach to introductory level psychology, tailor-made to the new modular style of teaching. Each short book covers a topic in more detail than any large textbook can, allowing teacher and student to select material exactly to suit any particular course or project.

The books have been written especially for those students new to higher level study, whether at school, college or university. They include specially designed features to help with technique, such as a model essay at an average level with an examiner's comments to show how extra marks can be gained. The authors are all examiners and teachers at the introductory level.

The *Routledge Modular Psychology* texts are all user friendly and accessible and use the following features:

- practice essays with specialist commentary to show how to achieve a higher grade
- chapter summaries to assist with revision
- progress and review exercises
- glossary of key terms
- summaries of key research
- further reading to stimulate ongoing study and research
- cross-referencing to other books in the series

For more details on our AS, A2 and *Routledge Modular Psychology* publications visit our website at www.a-levelpsychology.co.uk

Also available in this series (titles listed by syllabus section):

Adulthood

Evie Bentley

Routledge
Taylor & Francis Group

LONDON AND NEW YORK

First published 2007
by Routledge
27 Church Road, Hove, East Sussex BN3 2FA

Simultaneously published in the USA and Canada
by Routledge
270 Madison Avenue, New York, NY 10016

*Routledge is an imprint of the Taylor & Francis Group,
an Informa Business*

© 2007 Psychology Press

Typeset in Times and Frutiger by Keystroke,
28 High Street, Tettenhall, Wolverhampton
Printed and bound in Great Britain by TJ International Ltd,
Padstow, Cornwall
Paperback cover design by Anú Design

This publication has been produced with paper manufactured to strict
environmental standards and with pulp derived from sustainable forests.

British Library Cataloguing in Publication Data
A catalogue record for this book is available from the British Library

Library of Congress Cataloging in Publication Data
Bentley, Evie, 1947–
Adulthood / Evie Bentley.
p. cm.
Includes bibliographical references and index.
ISBN 0–415–25823–5 — ISBN 0–415–25824–3 1.
Adulthood—Psychological aspects. I. Title.
BF724.5.B46 2007
155.6—dc22   2006020887

ISBN: 978–0–415–25823–4 (hbk)
ISBN: 978–0–415–25824–1 (pbk)

With affection and gratitude to the Rockin' Rons and Doowoppa Doreens who modelled adulthood for me in my youth; and to all the other adults who have been influences whether as positive or negative role models: thank you!

Contents

List of illustrations

Tables

Figures

Box

Acknowledgements

Cara Flanagan and the people at Routledge including Lucy Kennedy and Tara Stebnicky for astonishing patience and encouragement; and my wonderful friends including the whole Downes family, Jill Keogh, Julia McLean, Nicola Meakins, Kristenne Pickles, Linnie Rawlinson, Ted Vallance, and my secret support crew, for the same.

Introduction to lifespan psychology

How this book is organised
What 'lifespan' means
Adolescence as the link from childhood to adulthood
Concept of adulthood
Methods of research
Summary

How this book is organised

The organisation of this book is in six chapters. First, there is this introductory chapter which looks at what psychologists mean by 'lifespan' and 'adulthood', and also at how this area of psychology has been researched. Chapter 2 deals with early and middle adulthood, and three important theories of human development during this time: the theories of Erikson, Levinson and Gould. Each of these theories views adulthood from a different stance, a different point of view, and these alternative approaches are all very interesting. Chapter 3 takes a fourth approach and looks at some of the main life events of adulthood, namely marriage and partnering, parenthood, and divorce from a psychological angle. Chapter 4 is about late adulthood, with sections on social psychological theories of ageing, the psychological effects of retirement and bereavement, cognitive changes in older adults, and some cross-cultural ageing studies. Chapter 5 has some alternative psychological perspectives on ageing, and Chapter 6 gives a senior examiner's comments on two student essays, showing where more marks could have been gained and therefore a higher grade obtained. This last chapter is a particularly useful one!

What 'lifespan' means

Lifespan psychology or development are relatively new terms. Psychologists used to refer to developmental rather than lifespan psychology, but the former term became equated with childhood development and so a new name was coined to include our psychological development throughout life. This is important, as it would be entirely wrong to imply that our personal, psychological development ceases at some point in the teens. We are dynamic individuals, and can and do continue to develop psychologically throughout life. Our environment and experiences continue to influence and perhaps shape us throughout adulthood.

Why was earlier research focused only on childhood? Well, several famous and influential psychologists thought that little or no further psychological development occurred after adolescence or from an even earlier age. Piaget felt that we developed stage by stage but once puberty had been gone though we remained wherever we were, psychologically speaking, for the rest of our lives. He did suggest an adult-type final stage, but went on to suggest that few of us reached it! You can read more about this in Lisa Oakley's *Cognitive Development* (Routledge 2004). Freud came from a different psychological direction, what we now call psychodynamic psychology, but he too felt that our psychological development was closely tied to childhood years, in fact to very early childhood. His fascinating theories are excellently described in Matt Jarvis' *Theoretical Approaches in Psychology* (Routledge 2000). Even the Behaviourists such as B.F.Skinner had one of their rare moments of agreements with other psychologists over this matter. Psychological development was not a concept they supported, as they considered any behavioural change to be the result of learning, i.e. responding to stimuli; and conditioning, classical or operant, as the mechanism for that change.

Adolescence as the link from childhood to adulthood

This stage in development is sometimes regarded as a western concept, an example of **ethnocentrism** and cultural bias. It is true that many other cultures do not have an intermediate stage between childhood and adulthood, meaning that adult life either begins on the day childhood ends or that there is such a gradual transition from childhood to adulthood so that adolescence is an irrelevant concept. But it is also true that in Eurocentric or western culture there is this intermediate stage starting from around the time of puberty, and this stage has been named and studied as adolescence. The psychology of this stage is covered in *Social and Personality Development* by Tina Abbott (Routledge 2001).

Concept of adulthood

This concept does not seem a difficult one until we try and define what we mean! It can be the time or age when a person has to take on legal responsibility for themselves – currently in the United Kingdom that would be on their eighteenth birthday. It can be when a person is judged mature enough to marry (16 years old in the UK), ride a small motorbike (16 in the UK, 14 in France) or buy alcohol in a public place (18 years old in the UK and 21 years old in the USA). Or it can be considered as reaching a state of maturity (Whitbourne and Weinstock 1979) – another term which is difficult to define! Whitbourne and Weinstock saw this as being happy to act responsibly, accept one's own social role, think logically, be emotionally aware, and cope reasonably well with life's smaller frustrations. Ten years later, Turner and Helms (1989) developed this particular theme further, adding that the mature/adult state promotes physical and psychological well-being by the person having sorted out their values, achieved a realistic self-concept, being stable emotionally and in relationships, and so on. Both these sets of ideas look very idealistic! I wonder how many of the over-eighteens in UK culture would agree that these describe their own behaviour. I suspect these criteria would disbar many people, perhaps even the majority, from being classed as adults!

Further difficulties are to do with the completely normal individual differences between people. Puberty itself is a moveable feast, and it is normal for this to start any time between the ages of 10 and 15 – or maybe in an even wider age range. If the biological clocks controlling this side of development vary so much, then it is not unlikely that psychological development also varies considerably and normally in its timing.

Another focus of individual differences is on the two sexes. It is true that most of the classic research, done in the twentieth century, focused on male psychological development. This is of course no surprise to anyone with knowledge of psychology. But we now acknowledge that we cannot just assume that because something has been researched in males we can apply the findings to females. There are similarities between the two sexes but there are also very important **gender differences**, and a great plus of current lifespan development research is that many researchers are clearly aware of this.

When psychologists research lifespan development they are today making several assumptions, as Sugarman (1986) has pointed out. We are individuals, with individual thoughts and individual choices – what he calls active agents in our own development – but we are also members of social groups such as our families, friends, school/college/work colleagues, neighbourhood. We have an impact on them and they on us, it's a reciprocal influence, and it's a dynamic one as well since relationships of any sort are rarely static. We are also, as human beings, highly complex creatures with highly complex brains and behaviours. No simple line of research and no simple set of explanations are ever going to be able to explain our development through life, even in distant years when lifespan development is no longer a new discipline.

Methods of research

This area of psychological development in adulthood has real research difficulties. Adulthood lasts such a long time, six decades and increasing, so that problems with good research build up fast. **Longitudinal studies** are by their very nature time-consuming and therefore very expensive. Also, people don't always stay put, and the original sample in such a study may be seriously depleted as some participants move away, lose interest in cooperating with the researchers, or die young. Another set of problems is to do with context as outlined above. A person's adult development will be closely linked with their cultural, social, political and financial context so that many different groups need to be studied if we are seeking a general picture of human adult development. A third group of difficulties comes with the \(\iota_{\jmath_{\rm r}}\) research methods being used. Researchers have their own ideas, otherwise they could not be doing the research. But if they are interviewing and observing people, the problems of validity, reliability and bias are bound to be there too. Ann Searle's book *Introducing Research and Data in Psychology* (Routledge 1999) has good sections on such research issues. And it is very hard indeed, some would say impossible (Popper 1969), for any human to be truly objective, especially when following their own ideas as in research, so we all need to be cautious in interpreting research findings.

So how old is 'old', and how adult are you? Probably we all know of younger people who seem set in their ways, old before their time; conversely we also probably know older adults who are busy in their minds if not physically and who have a lively interest in things. Kastenbaum (1979) suggested that we have several 'ages' (see Table 1.1 below) with which we coexist, and this certainly has face validity as so many people report acting or feeling older or younger than their years, depending on what they are doing and so on. One 2001 issue of the UK magazine for retired people, *Saga*, put a photo of the ageing rock musician Mick Jagger on its cover, which resulted in much amusement – and also a statement from Mr Jagger's team that they were 'horrified' at the photograph's use. This supports the view that adulthood and perhaps older adulthood is a concept interpreted differently by different groups of people.

Table 1.1 Kastenbaum's types of age	
Chronological age	This is how many years you have lived
Biological age	This is how old your body seems to be, it's the sort of shape you are in physically
Subjective age	This is how old you actually feel yourself to be
Functional age	This is the age associated with your job or role, your responsibilities, etc.
Social age	This relates to the age-group you mix with, how others see you, your personal 'style'

Try and think of people who you have read about, seen on TV or know, and map their 'ages' according to the table on the previous page. Try and think of one whose 'age' will vary. And do your own 'ages' agree, or do you have some variation too?

How useful do you think Kastenbaum's idea is?

Summary

- Lifespan psychology covers the psychological development throughout life;
- This idea of continual development is not held by some psychologists or approaches such as Piaget, Freud and the Behaviourists;
- Adolescence may be a culture-dependent stage in psychological development, specific to western-based cultures;
- Adulthood is difficult to define as many ideas, such as Whitbourne and Weinstock's or Turner and Helms', are idealistic rather than realistic and do not allow for individual differences in development;
- Researching psychological development is full of difficulties such as researcher bias and all the problems of researching by asking questions, e.g. validity and reliability;
- Kastenbaum suggested a set of age categories based not just on the number of years lived but on Biological, Subjective, Functional and Social Age as well. This allows for the individual and group differences we see around us.

Further reading

http://epunix.biols.sussex.ac.uk/Home/Julian_Staddon/age.html has useful links to sites on ageing.

Bee, H. and Boyd, D. (2002) *Lifespan Development*, 3rd edn, Boston, MA: Allyn & Bacon, is the latest edition of a classic text.

2

Early and middle adulthood

Introduction

Several classic theories have viewed our psychological development as a series of stages. These stages may be seen as crises, challenges, conflicts, seasons, transitions or transformations. Although this sounds somewhat uninviting, daunting even, people manage to get through adulthood and most of us even enjoy ourselves much of the time!

This chapter will look at the three most well-known theories of early and middle adulthood, and at relevant research studies plus critical discussion and commentary.

Erikson's conflicts theory

This theory is often known as the 'eight ages of man'. Erikson was originally a follower of Freud, i.e. he came from a psychodynamic background, but he did not agree with Freud's theory that the psychological development of the personality is complete when we become adult. Freud suggested that such development takes place mainly in childhood, and in early childhood at that, and suggested that this development was largely driven psychosexually. He proposed four main stages of psychosexual development – oral, anal, phallic and genital – combined with a tripartite development of the personality: the id, ego and super-ego. You can read much more about these interesting ideas in Tina Abbott's book in this series, *Social and Personality Development*. This theory of Freud's assumes that psychological development rarely if ever continues into adulthood. Erikson disagreed, and proposed that development is life-long and is not so much powered by sexual forces as by social ones, which is why this theory is sometimes called *Erikson's theory of psychosocial development.* He produced a plan of eight psychosocial stages (see Table 2.1) which he believed we work through during our lifetime. Moving on from one stage to the next was, he suggested, dependent on the individual resolving a personal, developmental crisis. Each crisis is based on a personal conflict such as a young adult's dilemma over resolving his/her desire for a close relationship with the fear of losing his/her own identity, which needs to be worked through and resolved before the individual person can proceed further, psychologically speaking.

Erikson's complete stages theory is outlined here so you can see how the adult stages follow on from earlier ones. This is to help your understanding of his approach, but do be aware that you only need to know the adulthood stages for this topic.

Adolescence and adult identity

Erikson suggested that the adolescent years would, if completed successfully from the psychological point of view, end with having developed the ability to see oneself as having a strong personal identity, in other words feeling confident about who and what one is. The person would have sorted out the adolescent confusions, and would be able to see themselves as having a consistent and integrated identity. This illustrates the crisis of adolescence, the resolution of which is the step into the identity of early adulthood.

Table 2.1 Erikson's eight stages of psychosocial development

Age	Life crisis	Description
1 year old	Trust v mistrust	A need to feel secure, rather than suspicious or fearful
2–3 years old	Autonomy v shame	A need for independence from parents rather than a lack of self-control or self-esteem
4–5 years old	Initiative v guilt	A need to explore, plan and be curious rather than be inhibited or guilty
6–11 years old	Industry v inferiority	A need to feel personally competent, and to achieve so that abilities are realised and not left undeveloped
12–18 years old (Adolescence)	Identity v confusion	A need to see oneself as an integrated person with a strong personal identity, both socially and sexually
20s and 30s (Young adulthood)	Intimacy v isolation	A need to experience both love and commitment personally and not be isolated
40s–mid 60s (Middle adulthood)	Generativity v stagnation	A need to be committed, concerned and caring about wide issues, and others in order to feel part of a wider whole, able to progress
65 years old + (Late adulthood)	Integrity v despair	A need to review life accomplishments, to feel satisfaction, acceptance of what has been and is, and not that life was wasted or not worth it

Early adulthood: intimacy versus isolation

The first crisis of early adulthood which needs solving is the conflict between intimacy and isolation. What this is all about is friendship and other close relationships – deep and lasting friendships where we trust others and reveal to them our true thoughts and feelings. Some of these friendships may develop from those of our teenage or child-hood years, some may be new. One or more of these friendships may develop still more and become romantic relationships, and/or erotic ones too. Erikson believed that as real intimacy involves sacrificing something of our own self we must have a strong or firm identity in order to be able to do this.

Of course, this stage can only happen if the previous conflicts of adolescence have been resolved and the person's sense of identity established. People need to have learned to give as well as take; to hold on to some things and to let go of others; to take initiative, to go for something or to play at it; to compete and to cooperate.

What is well known from painful, personal experience is that even surface friendships or relationships may bring us conflicts and nega-tive emotions. We must all have had the unhappy experience of telling someone we thought of as a friend something personal, maybe some-thing over which we felt vulnerable. And they go and spill the beans around – and we are hurt. This can happen at any stage of life, but in early adulthood Erikson suggests we explore our own ability to commit ourselves to others, to estimate and risk this disappointment and hurt, while coming to terms with having to make compromises of various sorts.

In early adulthood people become more realistic about themselves, their own abilities, their charms! Most realise that the chances of becoming a rock or film star are receding fast (if indeed those chances ever existed), and that taking over the world or becoming a millionaire are just pipe-dreams. People also cease to think that they may meet and become romantically involved with their icons – they acknowledge the harsh light of the adult day. They also become much more real-istic, and adapt to knowing that they cannot have things always their way. As you know, if we want to be friends with others, if we want to be loved, we have to consider the wants, needs and feelings of others, and compromise. The estate agents' mantra may be 'location, location, location' but for the young adult the chant should really be 'compromise, compromise, compromise' if relationships of most kinds are to progress and be rewarding. What this tendency also tells us is that the desire for an intimate relationship must be a basic one, a need as well as a want, for us to risk so much in its pursuit.

Intimacy versus isolation summarised

• Erikson proposed that early adulthood, the twenties and thirties, involves a crisis between intimacy and isolation, and intimacy is only possible after the identity crisis has been resolved in adolescence;
• This crisis must be resolved in order for the person to move on;
• This intimacy crisis is resolved by understanding ourselves in a realistic way, so we can build close friendships and experience intimate relationships;
• This enables the person to develop and mature psychologically;
• If this crisis is not resolved then the person will experience only superficial not meaningful relationships and this means that s/he becomes socially isolated;
• This will lead to minimal further psychological development as s/he will not be able to progress on to the next stage, middle adulthood.

Middle adulthood: generativity versus stagnation

The main focus of development here, according to Erikson, is the personal determination of what life is all about – what goals one has, what aims can be achieved, and how one can contribute to one's bit of the world. Erikson called this concept **generativity**. True generativity looks outside the family circle and considers our society and even world society, and how our descendants, the future generations, will live. This means generativity is not restricted to people in middle adulthood but is shown by anyone working for the future and the future good. Environmentalists as well as parents; child psychologists as well as some political or business people; these show generativity because they are working for a better future for the community. Erikson suggests that if this generativity is achieved, the person will find they can build clear guidelines for life, clear standards as to what should and should not be done, and that this will make that person not only happier but also able to live a productive life.

This may all sound very idealistic, but perhaps humans do actually have ideals though we may not always talk about them openly. It may be a rosy idealised image of humanity, or it may surely be true that we want something better, want to make our bit of the world better too – and even leave it, eventually, a slightly better place. Most people with families also want to hand on better things to the children, whether better in a material way or in other senses.

The alternative, if generativity is not achieved, is stagnation. Stagnation is the state of acting like a child, self-centredly, selfishly, demandingly, in a refusal to 'grow up' and accept adult life and its responsibilities. This can seem amusing as a fantasy – adults on skateboards, at pop festivals, 30-somethings (or older!) still experimenting with relationships, sex, alcohol, and so on – but in reality it could perhaps be not so amusing, and seems actually to be happening to sections of the community, and is known psychologically as perpetual adolescence. Sheehy (1996) suggests that for many who can afford it early adulthood is now delayed till the 30s or 40s. This lengthening of an early stage need not be a disaster, need not be actual stagnation, and could be an example of the effects of changing social norms. But both psychologists and sociologists have predicted problems. For instance, when such 'Peter Pans' do produce families they may still think of themselves in an adolescent way and therefore still challenge instead of provide authority. This could mean they find themselves emotionally at a loss in their guiding role as a parent, and they may even look to their own children for stability and structure in life instead of providing this. The media have portrayed examples of this sort of situation, and probably the most famous and certainly the most amusing are Patsy and Edina in the classic TV series *Absolutely Fabulous*. And I am sure you can think of at least one pop/rock or media star who might fit into this concept!

Generativity versus stagnation summarised

- Erikson suggests the crisis of middle adulthood, the 40s, 50s and early 60s, is between generativity and stagnation;
- Generativity is where the adult invests in a socially responsible future such as building family, community and career;
- Stagnation is where the adult focuses only on the self and personal wants and is self-centred, selfish in outlook and behaviour;

- A successful resolution leads to a sense of achievement and involvement in the future;
- This means the person will be able to move on and develop further, psychologically;
- Failure to resolve this crisis would produce feelings of dissatisfaction, personal impoverishment, of going nowhere;
- This would mean that the individual is held up in this stage and is unable to progress further, psychologically.

Evaluation of Erikson's theory

One important advance in Erikson's thinking in comparison to Freud was that he believed that personality continues to develop throughout life and is not set for ever by the late teens, as Freud suggested. A second advance is that he saw people as driven by more needs than just the physical/sexual ones – powerful though these may be.

Individual differences and gender

However, Erikson was, as many psychologists have also been, taking a biased viewpoint. He had meant to produce a universal theory which could apply to humans of both sexes, in any social or cultural context. But, as he himself came to agree, his interpretation of personal development was very male-focused. He based his ideas on his own generation of mainly males, and other researchers have found evidence that females may often progress through Erikson's stages in a different way to males. This gender variation is a basic example of individual differences, and it is now well acknowledged that there will be differences between males and females as well as between different males and between different females in when and how they resolve the two personality crises. For instance, Gilligan (1982) is one of several who have pointed out that in our own society males usually achieve identity before going on to gain intimacy, whereas for many females the two, identity plus intimacy, are achieved together, or the establishment of identity may be put on hold. Traditionally in western culture men would wait till they had progressed in the world of work before committing themselves to an intimate relationship with responsibilities whereas this was not so for women, which might also explain the social norm of a wife being younger than her husband. This may be due to the traditional view of a woman being important for her role, such as friend or wife, more than for her true self. Hodgson and Fisher (1981) studied a sample of woman undergraduates and found that most who were rated as identity achievers (from adolescent stage) also had achieved intimacy, though half of those who were not identity achievers had also achieved intimacy. What might this mean? It could be that women achieve intimacy before identity, in other words females might resolve this stage in the opposite order to males. This idea is supported by Sangiuliano (1978) who suggests that, tradition-ally at any rate in our society, a woman has sublimated her own identity into that of her partner. So, though she may have achieved intimacy, the search for her own identity may be suppressed until mid-life or later. This emergence may be what others call her mid-life crisis, as her search for identity and perhaps independence blossoms. Livson's (1981) data from the Oakland Growth Study which began in 1934 seems to support this late-blossoming. She compared those who had during adolescence been classed as traditionals with the non-traditionals. At age 40, the traditionals were resolving the issue of intimacy and by age 50 they were in the generativity stage. The non-traditional women appeared to be having a mid-life identity crisis at age 40, a throwback to adolescence as they seemed to be unsure of their identity and role. This did not hamper development because they went on to be the best adjusted at age 50.

Cultural differences

It seems that Erikson's theory is also quite culture-specific, quite Eurocentric. It is a common but faulty assumption that what goes on in our own, western and industrialised culture is a model for all people; but that view is a legacy from the more ignorant and biased time of the mid-twentieth century and earlier. Erikson's model could hold up well for some people but it does not fit in so well with other groups from other cultures or other socio-economic groups. Neugarten (1975) pointed out that in lower socio-economic groups, what he called the working classes, the key developmental stages of early adulthood happen a great deal earlier than for the higher socio-economic groups. He was focusing on males, but in this case female development would logically be comparable, when he pointed out that for the former 'working-class' group identity and intimacy were achieved by the early

20s when these groups would go into full-time employment, marry, settle down and raise families; whereas for the latter, higher socio-economic group males this would happen a decade later. In this new century and millennium it seems that, for our society, later achievement of this stage is far more the norm.

Studies of other national groups have also shown variations. Many of us will know of the struggle against apartheid in South Africa, and the establishment of a more multicultural society initially under the leadership of Nelson Mandela. Under the old regime most black people had difficult social conditions to cope with, such as poor housing and educational opportunities, poor medical care; and underpinning all this their low social status. With this struggle for existence it is not surprising that researchers found that, compared to the white population, the black people had a difficult time achieving a sense of identity and intimacy before late adulthood (Ochse and Plug 1986). More recent research gives the hope that, with social conditions changing in RSA, 'whole groups of blacks may expect to experience a completely different psychological development' (Price and Crapo 1999). A different black culture comes from, for instance, parts of the West Indies and Black America where it is the norm in some societies for men to sire children with a number of women (Alibhai-Brown 2000). The concept of identity and intimacy is clearly different here, established by a person's culture rather than a national group which is often made up from a mix of cultures. Erikson suggested a universal theory of adult development but it may be that progression through adult life is culturally rather than innately determined.

Empirical evidence

Unfortunately, Erikson's theory has been criticised as partly conjecture because it was not based on a body of empirical research and therefore lacked firm scientific evidence. He used earlier research but this was largely not testable or refutable, such as clinical evidence gained as a practising psychoanalyst, and reflections on interviews with the Dakota Indians, and on detailed biographical case studies, such as those of Gandhi and Martin Luther, as well as more ordinary people. But unfortunately Erikson's theory does not lend itself to empirical research and without hard, empirical evidence a theory is supposition and this can reduce its credibility.

This need not be an insurmountable problem – Freud's theory had the same conjectural basis and yet he is probably the most well-known psychologist in the world even though he is criticised for the lack of scientific evidence, and what evidence he did have consisted of biased case studies.

On the other hand this theory does have some face validity as it ties in with what we see and, for many if not most of us, what we feel about early and middle adult behaviour and development. This is supported by McAdams *et al.*'s (1993) study where middle adulthood people's responses showed generative concerns.

Conclusion

Erikson's theory has many interesting and stimulating ideas, primarily that we go through adult life in a series of stages, and we can only move on from stage to stage if the crises of each stage are resolved. However, there are many and varied individual differences, so each crisis and its resolution is variable in its timing and/or sequence from person to person. And social forces such as gender and socio-economic group are also vitally relevant in determining the pattern of development. So overall Erikson's pattern is an outline pattern only, the details being determined by the society in which the individual person lives.

Levinson's transitions theory

Levinson named his theory the Seasons of a Man's Life (1978; 1986) and though his is really a stage theory he preferred the term 'seasons' because he felt 'stages' imply that early ones are inferior to later ones, and in the developmental context that was not his vision. He felt that each season is appropriate for its time in life, and later ones are not better, just different, as the person is older. He also felt that although each person is a unique individual yet all follow a basic plan or pattern through life, which he termed the **life structure**. He called this pattern the seasons of a man's life and suggested that our **life cycle** fits a sequence of four main periods or seasons (see Table 2.2). His theory suggests that early adulthood's season is from approximately 17 years to 45 years, and middle adulthood goes from about 40 years to 65 years. The overlapping years from 40 to 45 he called a transition, and the **transitions** from one life stage to the next are a key feature of the

Age	Season	Description
Table 2.2 Levinson's seasons of a man's life		
0–16 years	Childhood and adolescence	
17–45 years	Early adulthood	Entering the adult world, becoming independent in a way which links the self and the adult world; which concept, together with ideas for the future, is called the Dream
40–65 years	Middle adulthood	Settling down, consolidating goals, commitments, etc., evaluating the Dream so far
60 years +	Older adulthood	Evaluating the pursuit and realisation of the Dream, accepting reality

Levinson theory. Each transition is a time of change, where the previous season is left behind, the life structure changes and the new season is embarked upon.

Early adulthood

This season runs from about 17 years old to about 45 years old.

Early adulthood transition

The transition from adolescence, which takes the first five years of this season, involves gaining independence and exploring personal possibilities. The person moves away from childhood dependence, for instance emotional and financial dependence, and explores the choices they have, such as their personal identity or self-concept and their occupation. This is not to say they have made their minds up about these things, but that they are thinking seriously about them. Many students in higher education are in this stage, making decisions about their next course or career move, about the sort of person they wish to be and how they wish to be perceived. They will have been thinking about these matters for some time, probably, but now they reappraise their earlier ideas and bring their current maturity to bear on them. The result of this is a personal construct named **the Dream** by Levinson. He uses this term to encapsulate a sense of where in life the person is going. It represents the life goals, career, relationship or otherwise, which that person has and for which they are aiming and planning, even if not fully aware of this.

Early adulthood: settling down

Then true early adulthood takes off, and in Levinson's view this is possibly the most dynamic period of adult life, and also the most challenging and stressful. This is because decisions are having to be made, though still leaving open possibilities for later on, also commitments given, and a firmer life structure emerges. Some dreams may become reality such as establishing a home of one's own, a stable relationship such as a marriage, a job promotion. But a sense of the years slipping by is also likely to be felt, and some decisions may have to be made now as they will not be available later on.

The early thirties transition

A smaller transition then takes place at around the age of 30. Readjustments are likely to be needed in life and in the Dream, and if the person manages to focus successfully on their own key concerns, and contributes positively to domestic, personal and occupational life they will be making themselves a secure niche in the adult world.

Generally, in the 30s, early adulthood's peak is reached and key components of the Dream are realised. This is often heavily influenced, and may be dependent on, the existence of a mentor, a rather specialised form of role model. This mentor is likely to be older, more experienced, perhaps a colleague or even the boss. Mentors provide vital encouragement and advice on how to go about achieving career advancement. This time of life also involves settling down with the various choices which the person has made, at home, at work and personally. This involves accepting responsibility for themselves in these areas as they have thought out what is important to them.

This has been called achieving BOOM – *b*ecoming *o*ne's *o*wn *m*an. The person is keen to build a better life and to be in some way creative and contribute to their community or to society; and in return they need society to recognise them as a positive contributor and achiever. Conflicting with this, though, is a desire not to be dependent on social norms, pressures or controls but to be able to be self-sufficient.

Early adulthood summary

- The early adult transition, from late teens to early twenties, involves the young adult constructing a vision which Levinson called the Dream of what and how they would like to be in the adult world;
- The Dream acts as a life plan, to guide, direct and motivate the person;
- If it is realistic it and its owner will flourish, but if it is unrealistic and unattainable it will fade away or die and the person will be left with a sense of lost purpose and a diminished sense of aliveness.

Middle adulthood

The middle adulthood season lasts from around the age of 40 to approximately age 60.

Mid-life transition or crisis

This season of course starts with the transition from early adulthood, from 40 to 45 years old, and the alternative name for the transition is the **mid-life crisis** as for some people this truly is a crisis time. The crisis is probably to do with the realisation that life is passing, youth is slipping away and one is only a mortal. People see that they are ageing, physically at least, and this is seen, in western culture at least, with regret. Why else is being told one looks youthful such a compliment; why else is the cosmetics industry selling so many, and such expensive, lotions and potions to delay the signs of age; why else is aesthetic (= plastic) surgeons' business booming? People want to be perceived as in their youthful prime, whether they are in early adulthood or not! But factors other than our appearance bring the reality of years passing in to confront us. Some people have to deal with facing bereavement, of friends or of parents. And each such loss is a sign, an intimation, of mortality – adulthood won't last for ever. People may see that their Dream will not now be achieved, and Levinson felt that if the Dream actually disappeared the person would lose their 'sense of aliveness and purpose'. To be successful the Dream may need further adjusting as decisions need remaking in the light of experience. Otherwise overwhelming disappointment may undermine the person's well-being.

However, not everyone experiences a mid-life crisis, and of those who do very many come out of it positively. The BOOM stage is completed in this transition, and middle adults are able to be like Friday's child in the old rhyme, loving and giving, so they are positive and reflective rather than stagnating and isolated.

Middle adulthood

Middle adulthood too can be a time of achievement, initiative and gain. Most people give up their illusions of being perpetually youthful, of immortality, and look outwards in a quite idealistic way. They look for ways to contribute to the good of the next and future generations. Some middle adults are people of influence and/or authority and can have power as well as the wisdom of their years to make long-lasting changes in their own group, community or on a wider scale. Perhaps we also want to leave something of ourselves behind, footmarks in the sands of time; and perhaps humans are also more willing to listen to people with an established track record. There may be significant life events such as divorce, and some middle adults may make a career change, or other personal changes, in effect going 'back to the drawing board'. Others maintain their Dream but adapt it subtly as their own attitudes or aims change and they become more kindly, more altruistic or deepen their personal attachments. Many people in middle adulthood say that it is the most rewarding, positive, productive and satisfying stage of life. These are the people who have their life and their self closely connected, probably through, in some way, restructuring their Dream.

The tasks Levinson suggests we have to complete to make middle adulthood successful involve reconciling four sets of opposing tendencies. These involve accepting not rejecting maturation; becoming more altruistic rather than self-seeking towards others and our community; developing emotional rather than worldly skills; and learning to understand our internal selves and needs instead of focusing on external achievement. So he suggests people need to find new ways of behaving so they can accept being older – giving up playing football or hockey perhaps, and taking up golf or walking. People also need to move on from more competitive and perhaps destructive behaviours, becoming more constructive and positive towards others. Levinson says men in particular need to accept and develop their feminine side and be more caring, creative and understanding towards others. Finally Levinson also suggests that men need to accept their inner self and reduce their drive towards career progress in order to get in touch with this inner man.

Middle adulthood summary

- Levinson's mid-life transition involves taking stock of life, of the Dream;
- It is a time of self-assessment, self-appraisal and looking again at what life means and holds in store;
- This can be a positive time; or if the Dream dies or is seriously threatened it can be an unhappy time, the mid-life crisis;
- For men in particular it can lead to a time of looking at inner development, rather than advancement in the world.

Evaluation of Levinson's theory

Empirical evidence

Levinson based his theory on his own research (1978). He analysed detailed interviews with forty American males aged between 35 and 45 years old, each participant being asked for an account of their own life, the key choices they had made and the consequences of these choices. The interviews took between 10 and 20 hours in total, over three months, and there was a follow-up two years later. These men were a non-randomly selected sample, ten each of biologists, novelists, businessmen and blue-collar workers.

Methodological criticisms

It is clear that this was a very biased sample, being only male and from a restricted age-range and backgrounds. This naturally means that the conclusions are not generalisable to the population at large, even the male half, so the research has limited application and use.

The retrospective nature of the interview also brings problems. With the best will in the world we know that memories are not factually correct recordings. How many times have you disagreed with another person over the recall of something both of you experienced? Often these disagreements are rather trivial, but we can get quite worked up because we think we are right – actually we know we are right! And yet we also know our memories have let us down many times in the past. This can affect our accounts of our lives. And another factor – we look back from our current viewpoint and interpret our past from where we are now. This is entirely understandable, but this can change the details of our personal histories, especially if we are talking about what choices we made, when and how and why. What all these points mean is that data gathered in this way cannot be said to have great validity; because of the various factors mentioned, a questionnaire, interview or survey may not in fact be measuring what it was intended to measure because, as Loftus has shown (1992), memories are reconstructed by the passage of time and subsequent experiences. In addition, we don't like to put ourselves in a poor light, we like to show ourselves at our best, a concept known as social desirability, and this also could reduce the validity of the data. All of this means that one should be cautious in drawing firm conclusions from these data because though they are rich they are not truly empirical.

Reliability is also a concern when using questionnaires. People's responses too often depend on their emotions, state of mind, and so on. For instance, when one feels rushed, under pressure, one may not give such full answers as when unhurried. If a person has been upset this will colour his/her perceptions and also interpretations even of memories. If they want to conceal something as they are not proud of what decision or choice they made, then people will do so especially if they are feeling insecure that day. This is real human behaviour and we've all been there! But from the point of research it has to be accepted that findings from questionnaires have low reliability though much breadth and depth, much richness, of information. So again one must be cautious in putting great dependence on the conclusions or the generalisations from such research.

On the other hand, the rich qualitative data obtained were directly about the actual experience of adulthood and had some face validity, i.e. they fit in with common sense and what we observe around us, and construct validity, i.e. they do seem to measure underlying themes in adult life; and the theory has been a useful stimulus for further ideas and research.

Other criticisms

The mid-life crisis is another contentious issue as there are no firm research data to support the idea. The many anecdotal examples of such crises in everyday life do provide some face validity but this concept is by its nature a very sensitive issue. This is because many mid-life crises are emotionally painful to both the person under-going the crisis and to those close to them, and great care would be needed to research such behaviours in an ethical and humane way. On the other hand, Valliant (1977) did a piece of research on male Harvard graduates, another highly biased socio-economic sample, and found that the occurrence of life crises – job changes, divorce, etc. – was no different in the 40s from any other time of life. Also we need to remember that some psychologists such as Erikson consider that adult life is a series of crises and not a set of seasons at all, so that if the mid-life crisis does exist it is but one of a series.

Research in women

Levinson (1986) later conducted a similar study with forty-five women as participants, producing much the same findings as the original study. Both Levinson's studies supported the idea of a common plan in the life cycle, with similar seasons and age-related transitions.

However, a well-known study by Roberts and Newton (1987) questions Levinson's results. They analysed detailed interviews with thirty-nine women. They found there was a gender difference, that the two sexes' life cycles or seasons are not closely comparable. They did find some similarities; most of the women they interviewed showed they had experienced a transition in early adulthood, between the ages of 17 and 22, and they did formulate their Dream during that stage.

But whereas men's Dreams were simple and mostly career-orientated, the women's Dreams were very complex involving combinations of career and other personal goals with interpersonal ones to do with relationships with other people, such as support for their 'special man'. This mixture of goals brought some conflict, but many women prioritised their goals, either pursuing the personal ones during their 20s and then changing their focus to the interpersonal ones, or vice versa. This research is certainly interesting, and can provoke useful discussion, but the very small and culturally biased sample means we cannot be certain of the validity of generalising from these studies to the population at large.

Conclusion

Of course, we all do follow a very basic plan through life – we are born, grow, mature, have relationships and eventually we die. But is this all that Levinson meant? Of course it's not. He was suggesting a theory of our individual, personal, psychological development as we go through life, applicable to all or nearly all of us. Unfortunately his research also demonstrates how psychology was focused on males as a model for us all, and this **androcentric bias**, a bias in favour of males, is not uncommon in psychology. This research was also based on mainly educated, higher socio-economic groups from traditional western or industrial cultures as participants, and so yet more bias was involved. This of course means that we have to acknowledge that Levinson's theory, which was intended as universal, has doubtful validity and application.

Gould's consciousness theory

Gould (1978; 1980) had a different vision of how we progress through adulthood. He started as a supporter of Freud's theories, but his work as a psychiatrist altered his views so that he saw the challenges of adulthood as a series of **separation anxieties** which needed to be dealt with in order to progress as human beings. He proposed that consciousness evolves throughout adulthood, and it is this change in consciousness which produces the adult personality changes. His theory was that we move through a succession of life stages where four, major, emotional **false assumptions** are addressed. The different

Table 2.3 Gould's four false assumptions		
Age	False assumption	Description
18–21 years	Parents and their world are right	The person will always belong to and believe in their parents' world and views
20s	Following the parents' way brings success	Parents know how to do things properly and well, and can advise/help successfully
30s	Life has simple rules and is controllable	The person is in control of life; mind and spirit and intellect are in tune; basically one is safe
mid 30s–50s	Problems have been overcome and life goes on for ever	Danger and death are unreal, family is real, the person has no guilt

assumptions are ones we, for a while, cling to as they seem to protect us from the vicissitudes of life; they create an impression of safety for us and protect us from separation anxiety. But this safety, Gould argues, is unreal, merely an illusion of absolute safety, and if we are to progress as human beings we need to face up to the anxiety, difficulty and perhaps even the pain of giving up these illusions and the assumptions on which they are based, precisely because they are false.

Gould believed that the path throughout adulthood was one of self-discovery, during which time we leave childhood ideas, standards and rules behind, together with our beliefs that parents are all-knowing and powerful. We discover that 'I', the individual person, is the main one who determines one's own life. We give up our comforting, former, false beliefs or assumptions, free ourselves from separation anxiety and change how we think of time.

Early adulthood

Gould saw the childhood consciousness as thinking, falsely, that the beliefs, standards and rules which determine much of a child's life were fixed, and would persist and govern the person's adult fate. He held that as the person moves into early adulthood, during the years from 18 to 21, they need to move away from these childish beliefs or assumptions.

What are these false assumptions which would need challenging? The main false assumption is that the emerging adult will still belong to and believe in their parents and the parental world, because:

- Parents are the only people who can guarantee one's safety
- Becoming more independent would lead to disaster
- Parental viewpoints are the only correct ones
- One can be a member of only the parental family group
- One's body is not one's own.

It's clear from the above that the problem which needs confronting is accepting that one may differ from one's parents or home background and their ideas and beliefs; and that any such differences need not be bad or wrong ones.

Teens into twenties

Then, as the person moves into their 20s, they need to overcome a wider set of false assumptions; the main one being that following one's parents' way is most likely to be successful, though it will need hard work, and if things don't go well one's parents will step in and help sort things out successfully, because:

- Parents know the one right way to do things
- Doing things properly, i.e. the parental way, always brings success
- If the person can't manage to do something themselves then one's parents and loved ones can always sort it out
- Keeping on trying one's best and being sensible will always bring better results than any other approach.

This too implies a struggle to gain independence from the parental home culture, and from assuming a position of lower personal knowledge and power.

Twenties into thirties

Then, as the person goes from late twenties to early thirties, the third false assumption takes over. This states that life is simple and controllable, and that there are no inner contradictions or conflicts, because:

- The person's emotional knowledge and their intellectual reason are in harmony
- One's parents were not always right and so in such specific areas one is not like one's parents
- One is able to see clearly the reality of the people around one
- There are no real threats to one's own safety.

This seems to mean that the person is in denial! It is as though the end of early adulthood brings a focus on what one would like to have as personal reality rather than the unwelcome truth.

Gould's early adulthood summary

- Gould saw adulthood as a journey of self-discovery;
- People need to challenge and leave behind sets of false assumptions which otherwise hold them back from being adult;
- This leads then to the realisation that they can, without being wrong or bad, differ from their parents or background in beliefs and ideas;
- This is a move to being independent and having personal knowledge and power;
- People need also to be realistic and pragmatic even if truths are unwelcome.

Middle adulthood

While Gould did not seem to put a division between early and middle adulthood, his next stage would clearly fit the latter. He proposed that from the mid-30s to age 50, if the previous three false assumptions have been successfully dealt with, the fourth one arrives. He considered this to be a particularly stressful time in life as we can no longer deny that the years are passing, that we have had half or more of our life-span, that we are mortal. However, this fourth false assumption denies these things as it says that evil and death do not exist, and threatening or unsettling things have been got rid of, because:

- A man's work, or a woman's work for a man, means that person is immune from any danger or even death
- The person's family is the only reality, the only life
- The person is innocent.

Once again this suggests the person is in denial, this time in denial of the unwelcome truths about life involving change, independence involving responsibility, and personal time having an end as well as a beginning.

Key concepts in Gould's theory

Trauma or normal?

One critical point about Gould's ideas on early adulthood is the implication that challenging one's parents' beliefs is a struggle! After all, in many of our own communities it is usually accepted that the teenage years are rebellious ones, and that it would therefore be the social norm for emerging adults to be disagreeing with their parents. On the other hand this overt rebellion is not actually true for many cultures including our own. There is research evidence which suggests that the idea of teenage 'storm and stress' is not in fact the norm, as most young people do not contest their parental culture, and in fact do accept their parents' ideals, beliefs and so on (Coleman 1978; 1980) without harm. A different way of looking at the inner conflict of adulthood could be that young adults need to find an internal *locus of control*, not an external one (Rotter 1966). This means that they start to see the central control of their lives as coming from within themselves so they have some power and influence for themselves, and not from outside themselves, for instance from parents.

Sense of personal time

Gould also suggested a different interpretation of his theory in a discussion of the sense of personal time flow. It is true that to a child a day can seem to last for ever, and 'next year' seem so far away as to be unimaginable. Even as we age, time changes its perceived speed and this change has now been identified as an actual change within the brain, due to its chemistry. Brain chemistry studies show that time is truly perceived as going faster for us as we get older. But to go back to Gould's point, even as teenagers we seem to have an infinite future stretching way ahead, out of view. But as we move through early adulthood this starts to change. Even when we are confident in our independence he suggests we still think that we are following a 'chosen path' and this will somehow lead us on to a bright future where we will get our rewards.

By the end of their 20s people see things a bit more realistically, time-wise. They still feel they have plenty of time to go, but are now aware of the adult past behind them as well. They realise they have to choose between different paths through life, that their life-line is not a straight line at all. They realise that some choices mean they can't do everything they want to do as there simply isn't enough time for all these things.

In the 30s people start to feel that time is no longer quite so much on their side, and during the 40s they realise time is beginning to run out. This could be a cause of the disputed mid-life crisis, if this really is a common experience. People also, Gould suggests, become aware of their own mortality, and once this realisation that time is finite is gained this stays in the consciousness. People therefore become increasingly more choosy as to how they spend their time, and he feels they now question whether their aims in life, their hard-won independence, have real value or are irrelevant. Coming to terms with such challenges means, according to Gould, that a person is in touch with her/his inner self, the inner core, and so feels that life has worth and meaning.

Evaluation of Gould's theory

Gould, like Erikson, was originally Freudian in his thinking, but his work as a psychiatrist caused him to change and to believe that the human personality continues to develop through life. His ideas about relinquishing what he termed false assumptions also ties in with childhood's **separation anxiety**, and he suggested that in order to achieve adulthood we have to challenge the desire to be as we were when children, emotionally attached to and looked after by someone else. His false assumptions seem to protect us from anxieties and fears and uncertainties, but as they are false this seeming safety is fiction – and Gould says we need to acknowledge this fact. If we were insecurely attached as children then this breaking away, challenging of false assumptions, might be harder than if we were securely attached as the latter would have developed confidence in ourselves.

Research evidence

Gould's original research was a sample of over 500 males, non-patients, between the ages of 16 and 50. They answered a questionnaire which he developed carefully with the assistance of medical students over several months. The students taped therapy sessions to provide material from which to devise the questions. The male sample were all from the upper socio-economic groups and all white. This research methodology immediately raises several issues of bias, like the methods of Erikson and Levinson. This, like much classic research in psychology, was white- and male-oriented and so is both culturally biased and androcentric. Therefore it is not truly representative of the general population, which means of course that even if the theory applies to white, high socio-economic males it cannot be generalised to other groups in the community. Additionally, Gould seemed to regard women as having reality or significance only in their roles relating to men (see middle adulthood false assumptions) and this attitude is now regarded as unacceptable as well as invalid.

Problems with questionnaires

The problems of data obtained from questionnaires and surveys are well known. There may be unforeseen *demand characteristics*, features of the questionnaire or how it was administered, which encourage participants to give certain responses and avoid others, possibly because they think they guess what the researcher is looking for. This is not a matter of deceitfulness, but rather of human-ness. We usually do like to please others and to do the 'correct' thing, and this has usually been socialised in us from early childhood! The researchers' close contact with participants in a survey may also lead unwittingly to interviewer bias as they unconsciously convey to their participants how they should respond, for instance in their tone of voice, facial expression or use of leading questions.

Extraneous variables are a main source of problems with questionnaires. We all know how we may change our opinions, or how we respond, depending on so many factors. Our mood; whether we are in a hurry, hungry, thirsty and so on; our motivation in answering the questionnaire; our state of mind; how we wish to be perceived (**social desirability bias**); whether the questions have been skilfully enough written for us to give a true answer; whether in fact we can recall very accurately what we are being asked about; whether we are in fact telling the truth at all – all these and many more variables could affect the results of the research. And if any of these variables are powerful enough they may become confounding variables as they, and not the parameters of the research design, determine the conclusions.

However, it is also true that with a good sample size (500), Gould's questionnaire would have provided a very rich source of data for analysis to generate rich knowledge about the sample. These data would have been representative of the population from which the sample was drawn, but not generalisable to a wider, socially and ethnically diverse population.

A final thought

Zeitgeist

The androcentric bias of much of this lifespan research has been mentioned earlier in this chapter. A further concern is the importance of looking at these theories in their own time context. This is separate from the cultural and socio-economic assumptions mentioned above. But while what they say about people might have been correct in those assumptions at the time, it is not likely to be so at the moment. Because of financial factors many young adults are not pursuing independence from their parental homes from the late teens, and many are staying put even when they are in employment. In many social groups the norms and the social pressures are no longer to establish a long-term, stable relationships during the 20s, and many adults delay settling down till well into their 30s. Of course there are cultural, sub-cultural and social variations to this, but the overall picture is different to the one of a few decades ago.

On the other hand, we in the west are now firmly in a culture where youth is all-important, as described in an earlier section. It is likely that when Erikson and Levinson were doing their main research the middle years were still thought of as the best years, the peak of life. Age used to bring respect for a person's experience, but that too has changed somewhat. Public perception, fostered by the media and advertising, puts youth above maturity, and social norms of what is good and desirable have changed as a result, and so people's Dreams and life plans may well have altered as well.

Summary

The main theories of early and middle adulthood focus on common life events and themes which it is suggested link together as a series of stages.

Erikson saw the stages as crises which had to be resolved if there was to be positive psychological development. The crises were intimacy/isolation followed by generativity/stagnation. But research evidence for his theory is not strong, and it did not acknowledge individual and cultural differences.

Levinson saw the stages as seasons with important transitions from one to the next. He did allow for individual differences in the rate of progression through the transitions, but as for Erikson's theory there is weaker, non-empirical evidence rather than hard empirical evidence.

Gould saw the stages as either a process of challenging false though attractive assumptions, linked to early childhood attachments, or as a journey with a changing perspective of time. He too, like Erikson and Levinson, based his ideas on weak evidence and a biased sample, and like Erikson did not allow for individual or cultural differences.

Further reading

http://www.hope.edu/academic/psychology/335/webrep2/crisis.html has recent research to do with the mid-life crisis.

http://www.mhhe.com/socscience/devel/common/middleadulthood.htm has useful links for this section.

Zimbardo, P., McDermott, M., Jkansz, J., and Metaal, N. (1995) *Psychology: A European Text*, HarperCollins, has an interesting chapter with discussions on the tasks, thinking and moral development of adulthood.

3

Family and relationships in adulthood

Introduction
The life events approach
Marriage and partnering
Parenthood
Divorce

Introduction

A very different approach to the study of adulthood is to look not at stages in development but at significant **life events** and how they can affect psychological development. The relevant main life events of early and middle adulthood are to do with making partnerships and marriages, parenting, and dissolving partnerships and marriages by divorce. A significant factor in these life events may be how much stress they produce, which might link in with psychological knowledge of stress, and Holmes and Rahe's Social Readjustment Rating Scale (SRRS).

The life events approach

The previous chapter looked at some of the stage theories of adulthood development. This chapter takes a different approach, that of looking at adulthood from the point of the main life events most or all of us

Table 3.1 Life events: ten examples from Holmes and Rahe	
Stressful life event	Life change units*/100
Death of spouse	100
Divorce	73
Marital separation	65
Marriage	50
Marital reconciliation	45
Pregnancy	40
Son/daughter leaving home	29
Trouble with boss	23
Change in social activities	18
Holiday	13

Note * Life change units are a measure of the stress associated with each event

experience. Some of these **life events** are stressful, as you may recall if you have studied Holmes and Rahe's (1967) research previously, but the amount of stress caused and indeed whether or not the events are actual stressors is a matter of individual differences. Three of the life events featuring on Holmes and Rahe's SRRS which are important, significant events of early and middle adulthood are partnering or marriage, parenthood and divorce. These events are bound up with the issues and concepts mentioned in one or more of the stage theories of Chapter 2, such as intimacy and relationships, independence, conflicts, emotions, personal responsibility and personal time passing.

Holmes and Rahe's work is often criticised from the methodological point of view. It was clearly not a concern in the 1960s or before that research should be male-based, male-biased in fact. Nor does it seem to have been a problem that the researchers accessed several thousand medical records looking for details of life events which preceded illnesses. In addition, their choice of such significant, stressful life events was highly subjective. For example a 'wife stopping or starting work' featured in their list, but there is no such mention of a similar event featuring 'a husband'.

From the modern point of view, it would also be necessary to approach this kind of research carefully, as many of these stressful events are socially sensitive and participants would need to be aware of their right to withdraw from the investigation and have their data destroyed, as well as being given an assurance of complete confidentiality.

We are also aware, today, that many events, such as divorce or losing one's job, could be extremely stressful – or give a relief and release from stress.

If you look at the table of life events you could discuss whether Holmes and Rahe's ideas about stressful events apply to you. If you are in your teens you may well feel that most of the events they considered as main life events are not yet in your personal experience, though you may be able to think about others that are stressful to you. This might also be a useful task if you have left your teens behind. Think about whether any of these stressful events have an effect on your behaviour towards others, especially friends and family. Could personal stress affect relationships?

Progress exercise

Marriage and partnering

The sharing of one's life and building of a shared future with a chosen, significant other person is what most of us envisage by the terms marriage or partnering. Every culture and possibly sub-culture has its own precise form of such an arrangement. In some cultures the two people concerned choose each other freely; in other cultures the choice may be partly limited, for instance by financial, cultural or social norms; in a few cultures the choice is made for the couple concerned by other people such as the family or parents. However, the fact that in most cultures people pair up, whether for a period of time or for life, indicates that this type of close relationship is innate in the human psyche.

The traditional western marriage has been the most investigated partnership between two people, with interest in both the *types* of marriage and the *themes* within a marriage as research areas.

Types of marriage

Cuber and Harroff's model

Five types of marriage were identified by Cuber and Harroff (1965):

1. Conflict-habituated marriages are the fighting relationships often depicted in the entertainments media. To outsiders the relationship seems one of constant strife, but in actual fact the two people involved have an implicit routine and understanding, and though the marriage seems stressful the couple would not in fact be thinking of divorce, and would probably not be happier if they did part.
2. Devitalised marriages are basically relationships based on routine; though the couple still profess love for each other they share few activities or interests and the marriage seems to be one of convenience, a comfortable habit, so it is presumably not worth the turmoil of changing or ending it.
3. Passive/congenial marriages also seem to be ones of comfortable habit and convenience, but here the couple do share contentment as well as each other's interests.
4. Vital marriages involve the couple sharing equally their involvement in and commitment to the joint and family activities such as the family finances, parenting, recreational interests and activities.
5. Total marriages are where the couple are totally bound up with each other in complete commitment, sharing personal, emotional and work confidences, fantasies even, as well as their family interests and organisation.

Interestingly, Cuber and Harroff considered marriage number 3, the passive or congenial marriage, to be rather undesirable, whereas now, forty years on, many people think of it as one with great positive potential; an example of the importance of seeing research in its own time context, perhaps. Another example of time context is the attitude to marriage number 5 which today could be regarded as confining, unhealthy and stifling of the essential and unique personalities of each member of the couple, whereas the term 'total' marriage seems to imply 'ideal'. A further psychological problem with this type of marriage is that by the parents focusing so closely on each other their children could be emotionally excluded. This means that children of such a marriage might suffer by being prevented from forming the normal, healthy, strong emotional parental bond or attachment which psychologists feel is the best predictor of a happy adult life.

Duberman's model

Eight years later Duberman (1973) produced a different set of three types of marriage:

1. Traditional marriages have the authority vested in the man, he is the responsible decision-maker except maybe in matters relating to children and domestic things. This view is exemplified in the old German saying of the proper duties of a woman/wife – 'kinder, kuchen und kirche' (children, kitchen and church).
2. Companionship marriages have an emphasis on shared decisions and responsibilities, on equality between the couple, and on companionship and satisfaction. Typically they do not divide things into male and female roles as either partner may be involved in any area of their shared life.
3. Colleague marriages also greatly emphasise sharing and personal satisfaction, but there are fewer sharing roles than in the companionship marriage. Instead the couple here accept role differences as each one takes responsibility for different parts of the shared life in line with their personal abilities and interests.

Research evidence

Research ideas of what and how matters are shared within a marriage have tended to focus on what is easy to quantify rather than what might be matters of important interest – housework, for instance, rather than attitudes or beliefs. The results of the research are hardly surprising! In the 1970s women spent more time than men on housework (Walker 1970), but husbands of working wives did more than husbands of non-working wives.

By the late 1980s there had been a small but significant change in beliefs about sharing tasks within marriage, in accordance with social changes. Though women were still considered to have overall responsibility for the home, in couples where both worked outside the home men did do more housework, but women really cut down on the housework they did, i.e. less housework overall was done (Presland and Antill 1987).

By the 1990s it was suggested that household tasks were being shared and divided depending on people's physical strengths and whether the work was being done inside or outside. For instance, the research category of 'housework' was abandoned and smaller categories were used. These showed that men might carry out dustbins, and wash cars, but women might do more cooking and cleaning (Matlin 1993). The idea that social trends determine this sort of partnership is supported by Wright *et al.* (1992), who compared American and Swedish men's contribution to housework. The male Swedes did considerably more in the home than the Americans, and this is attributed to the Swedish commitment since the 1970s to gender equality in several areas such as childcare provision, taxation and family support. Such a government commitment can lead the way to changes in personal behaviour, perhaps an example of minority influence at work, but this commitment has not been seen in the USA or indeed in other European countries.

Commentary on research evidence

The problems inherent in the research methods used in researching early and middle adulthood are also found in researching marriage/ partnering. Much research into types of marriage has been done using interviews and questionnaires, and the drawbacks to these methods are well known; they have been discussed, along with the difficulties of true objectivity and bias, in the preceding chapter.

Both Cuber and Harroff's and Duberman's models of marriage are not only **Eurocentric** but also 'children of their times'. First because they were only looking at their own quite narrow community in formulating the models, an approach which was the norm for most researchers then, they unwittingly were ignoring most of humanity. Secondly, in the last three decades there have been great changes in social organisation and norms in most western societies and this is of course reflected in social institutions such as marriage. Another point is that virtually all systems of categories have the same flaw – generally the categorisation seems to make good sense, but when we look at individual cases, such as an individual partnership or marriage, a couple will rarely fit completely and perfectly into any one category. This means that the **validity** of such classifications is rather weak. It also seems likely that marriages are not fixed in stone, as it were, but are **dynamic**. They are, after all, human relationships and would change and evolve as the persons in them develop. So it is quite probable that even if a couple does fit neatly into a category at one point in their history, they may move into another category at another point. This would cast doubts on the **reliability** of the categorisations, unless the categories were 'snapshots' at a point in time and, if repeated at intervals, could show any change in the relationship. This would mean that the categorisation becomes a useful research tool for describing how relationships change.

However, we humans do have a clear preference for wanting to group similar or fairly similar things together – witness the number of people who are collectors – of coins, books, toys, antiques and so on! And grouping similar relationships together could be a useful research strategy. It could bring a greater chance of discovering interesting common features which might otherwise be overlooked. This means that it sometimes can be, after all, useful to classify marriages.

Gender differences associated with marriage

In 1972 Bernard published findings which showed that married men are more psychologically stable as well as healthier and happier than single men are, and even than married women. This study confirmed earlier results from Veroff and Feld (1970).

Argyle (1983) has argued that a close, trusting relationship is the best basis for a happy marriage. This view is supported by Bee (1994) and Rutter and Rutter (1992).

The key issue here seems to be the increased social and emotional support which marriage usually brings. Argyle and Henderson (1985) have suggested this link as research showed such a clear tie between better mental health and marriage for both men and women. Schwarzer and Leppin's (1992) meta-analysis of 70 studies showed a small correlation, −0.22, between depression and social support. The problems here are first that a depressed person may well have a faulty perception of what social support they in fact do have; secondly that this may be one of those 'which came first, the chicken or the egg?' situations. Because depressed people are only seen after they have developed the depression, it is not possible to say whether the lack of social support was a partial cause of the depression, or whether it melted away as a result of the depressed person's behaviour.

Women provide better social and emotional support for their husbands than vice versa. This may be because of some innate gender-related trait, or it may be caused by ordinary socialisation. Taylor *et al.* (2000) found that women are likely to respond to stress with a 'tend and befriend' response, whereas most males would not do this. Further possible causes for the generally reported lower satisfaction of women within marriage could be because many women experience conflicts between their domestic role and their career or job; and if there are children then most women usually have to make a greater adjustment to their lives than their husbands have to. In fact, at least in traditional western marriages, greater adjustments have had to be made in self-acceptance and dominance by women than by men. And the greater reported male satisfaction in marriage is supported by the fact that following divorce, male rates of re-marriage are greater than female, over 75 per cent as compared to 65 per cent. Males seem to want the married state more than females do, though the difference is not huge. What is not clear is whether this greater preference is because men want to be cared for, or whether being able to have a wife is a male status symbol, or because of an entirely different set of reasons.

However, satisfaction in marriage has been assessed by self-reporting, so these data have low validity. Also, it is usually accepted that in our culture women are more open in accepting and expressing their emotions, and it is therefore possible that the apparent difference in satisfaction is just the result of this different willingness to express feelings. So men's greater satisfaction may be a false concept as it may stem from male difficulties in facing and acknowledging the reality of negative emotions and experiences.

Cultural differences associated with marriage

It is very obvious that psychologists have, in the main, been researching western-style marriages and neither those of other cultures nor of partnerships. It is true that researching same-sex partnerships would have been very sensitive and difficult while such relationships were outside the law, but in many countries these couples have been accepted, legally and increasingly socially, for some time.

Western married couples' satisfaction with their marriages has the pattern described above, with greater male than female contentment

(Schumm *et al.* 1998). However, the comparison with, for instance, Japanese couples' satisfaction has shown an important methodological problem. The criteria used for judging satisfaction in the two cultures were not the same because what the different cultures consider to be important in the relationship was not the same (Kamo 1993). This does illustrate a very important case for caution when making apparent comparisons, in other words researchers need to be sure their data are comparable, and in the Japanese and USA comparison study it seems there are doubts that they really were comparable. Though in both cultures marriage and the quality of the married relationship were regarded as very important, the significant factors differed. For instance, the size of the husband's income was a more important criterion for Japanese wives than American wives, and this may be because of the strong emphasis put by Japanese culture on perceived status. An interesting finding was that in Japan marital satisfaction remained stable with age, whereas in America there was a negative correlation between those two variables. This means that Americans felt less satisfied with their marriage as they grew older, but as this is a correlation then we cannot infer causation – other variables such as health and fitness, or reduced opportunities, may have been the actual cause of general satisfaction reducing as people aged.

Levine *et al.* (1995) looked at marriage in eleven cultures on five continents. They found that a key factor was the type of culture. Most western, industrialised cultures are individualist as the important focus is on people as individuals, and individual talents, progress and achievement are valued. In many non-western cultures people are seen as valuable because of what they can bring to the group, their family, extended family or community. This type of culture is known as **collectivist**. In **individualist** cultures the uniqueness of each person is valued. Each is important because each is an individual. These cultures put emphasis on love within a marriage, as do cultures with higher material standards of living, lower birth rates, and higher marriage and divorce rates. Collectivist cultures see a person's importance as being part of their group – which may be their extended family – as well as of their whole culture. These cultures do not see romantic love as important, rather they put the importance of the social group, society, as the key factor in a marriage. This sort of culture has traditionally had high birth rates and lower marriage and divorce rates but less focus on material possessions.

41

Box 3.1 A traditional Egyptian marriage

An example of this collectivist culture is the traditional Egyptian way of life, not as seen today in cities such as Cairo but in what is still called Upper Egypt, the southern half of the country (Dergham 2001). This area has not been exposed to foreign cultures and so has maintained until very recently its characteristic Seidi lifestyle. Here it is very different from western, industrialised life. Boys and girls do not mix or even meet freely. Meeting places, places for entertainment, do not exist. So making a marriage depends on other things, one of which is El-Khatba, the marriage broker, usually an old woman with wide social contacts. She will suggest suitable unions if the family itself is unable to find a match within its relations. Factors which are considered important are the financial, social and religious position of the respective families and this ties in with the collectivist approach. Each person, and therefore each marriage, is important most of all because of its significance within the family group, usually what we call the extended family. Dergham reports one case study of a Seidi woman, a vegetable seller, whose marriage is typical of her culture. This woman's father told her a month before her wedding that she was engaged to be married and the ceremony would be in one month's time. The prospective groom had paid a dowry in money and gold jewellery, and the bride's father had promised his daughter plus all the furniture and other things needed to set up the new home. The marriage celebration lasted one week, with the actual ceremony as the final part when the bride and groom became husband and wife, and the men and women did not mix during all this but sat in separate groups. Speaking at a later time, looking at her married life, this wife is proud that she is a good wife according to Seidi custom, caring and supportive towards her husband as well as being a good mother. She also comments that in the past decade or so things even in Upper Egypt are beginning to change. Many women do not do paid work, and spend a lot of time watching television or listening to the radio. What they hear and see has altered their perception of what life has to offer. Indeed, it is possible that the government in its drive to promote education, health and fewer pregnancies has overtly supported this enlarging of their world. The modern young people may change their behaviours and attitudes to, for instance, choosing a marriage partner, as a result.

The effects of marriage on the individual

In current western culture the statistics show, amazingly, that over 90 per cent of adults marry, once at least. This is surprising, for the comments from the media suggest that marriage is out-dated; that it is a failing institution; that it is rejected by many especially the 30-something generation; that divorces outnumber marriages. But even though social changes are constantly happening it must also be true that marriages are still taking place and that almost everyone will at some point be married. Psychology has therefore asked the question – why? Why in this day and age of supposed personal independence and opportunity do people continue to join themselves in marriage with another? Possibly because it is a visible sign of adult status; hopefully it brings intimacy, companionship and emotional security as described by Erikson; it is an accepted unit in which to produce and raise a family. These are all positive and productive aims. The overall answer seems to be that we believe, with some reason, that marriage, not just living with a partner, will make us happier – an excellent goal!

Research evidence about the effects of marriage

Bradburn's (1969) research in the United States showed a big difference in self-reported happiness levels between unmarried people, 18 per cent of whom felt they were very happy, and 35–38 per cent of married people who judged themselves as very happy. Separated or widowed men were the most negative with only 7 per cent saying they felt very happy. Bradburn also asked if participants were 'not too happy'. Here also the data supported marriage as the best option; 40 per cent of separated people, 30 per cent of divorced people, 17 per cent of never-been-married people but less than 10 per cent of married people reported being not too happy.

Later research by Argyle and Furnham (1983) confirms the model of marriage as leading to increased happiness. They investigated factors which people find important in making a relationship happy or satisfying, and they found three. These were material and instrumental help (meaning actually giving either help or something which was needed); social and emotional support; and having common interests. Though friends and others in non-sexual relationships with the participants were rated as important, spouses were rated higher in all three factors but especially better in giving material or instrumental help. A more recent questionnaire study by Argyle (1990) still backs up the marriage-gives-more-satisfaction hypothesis. He found that married people:

* Take better care of their health, e.g. they drink and smoke and get drunk less, and follow medical advice better
* Are less likely to need in-patient treatment
* Have a healthier immune system.

This may be due to the psychological benefits of mutual support, and avoiding isolation, and perhaps also to the beneficial exposure to more germs than one's own or workplace pathogens!

One overall finding about marriage and satisfaction/happiness has suggested that a marriage starts off with high levels of positive emotions, but these levels drop in mid-adulthood. They then pick up again in late adulthood (Swenson, Eskew and Kolheff 1981; Bengston *et al.* 1990). Bee (1998) has confirmed this model of a U-shaped satisfaction curve.

This, the accepted model, has been challenged for instance by Valliant and Valliant's (1993) longitudinal study. This has followed the marriages of 169 Lebanese college women and men over forty years. The Valliants' research suggests that marital satisfaction remains

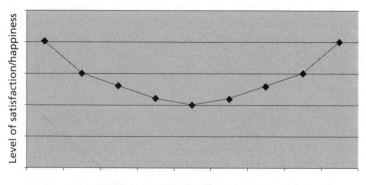

Time in years

Figure 3.1 **Frequency curve showing changes in satisfaction/happiness during marriage**

fairly stable through time, though the stresses and strains of marriage obviously will vary, especially if bringing up children is involved. They used a prospective approach, where people were asked for their feelings about the current situation and its future, and then at some later time checked their views again. This method could give more robust, more valid data because in such a longitudinal study the same participants are being tracked through their life changes so their data comes from them directly and not on researchers' guesses or opinions about the participants. Furthermore, their research is both interesting and encouraging, albeit culture-specific. Former researchers have used the retrospective approach with all its known pitfalls such as reconstructive memory and forgetting, so that participants' recollections about how they felt or what they experienced in previous years are faulty, not reliable. It is possible that people may recall the physical, mental and financial costs of running a young family better than the joys and rewards and excitements. Sleep-deprived nights, the perceived cultural pressure to be super-mum or -dad, the genuine, deep desire to give one's children the best possible start in life – all these things are potent stressors and may be remembered all too well. On the other hand, another problem could be just with the sample. Marriages found to be unsatisfactory may have ended during middle adulthood, and so in the late adult cohort they do not appear – hence this later sample seem happier, more satisfied, by comparison with the middle sample. What does all this research seem to tell us? Overall, it seems that married people are happier than unmarried people. This happier state varies with time, being high in the early years of the marriage, dipping after a few years and then if the marriage still exists increasing again in late adulthood.

Marriage and mental health

Earlier in this chapter it was pointed out that marriage seems to improve physical health and longevity. There is also research to show it also protects our mental health. This is not to say that single people are likely to go mad, nor that being single causes mental disorders, but there does seem to be a link between marriage and good mental health. Gove (1979) found that married people had far lower rates of mental disorders than their single peers. This was confirmed by Cochrane (1988) who looked at admissions to mental hospitals. The rate for married people was 0.26 per cent whereas the rate for single people was 0.77 per cent. However, Gove was only looking at those with serious mental disorders who needed treating as in-patients. There is a far larger number of people whose mental disorders are treated by their family doctor and who may never be seen in a psychiatric clinic or ward. The relevance of this here is that research has shown that people high in social support, such as married people, report a third fewer symptoms of distress even when highly stressed compared to those with low levels of social support (Cohen and Hoberman 1983). In low-stress situations there was no difference in physical symptoms between the two groups. Of course, factors such as the type and amount of support, the accessibility of support and the emotional closeness of the support-giver(s) are also very relevant (Thoits 1982). But for most people, support from the nearest and dearest person, the spouse or partner, would surely be the most valuable and this could be what protects these people's mental health when they are married.

Commentary on research into the effects of marriage

Today we have to bracket partnership and marriage together as, for younger people at any rate, living as a partnership or cohabiting is openly acceptable for heterosexual couples as well as for same-sex couples. Yet most psychological research is still focusing on marriage, perhaps because of methodological difficulties such as identifying cohabiting couples in a convenient locality, or perhaps because about 60 percent of cohabiting couples progress into marriage.

Much research into the effects of marriage has used questionnaires and surveys, and these research methods' problems exist here as elsewhere. Researching by asking participants questions does give rich data and that is a strength. But the inability to tell whether the responses from participants are truthful, or how truthful they are, is a real issue. In this area of research, that is, marriage in general, and mental health and marriage, people might well have felt it important to present the best possible picture of themselves and their relationship. They may have felt some reservation at being very open with the researchers, and the subject matter was extremely personally as well as socially sensitive. We also cannot know quite how the researchers interpreted participants' answers, and whether interviewer bias was a factor here. And most of the research described above also ignores the natural individual differences between us all. Some of us are naturally optimistic, others pessimistic. Some of us find satisfaction more easily than others do. We also go through happier and less happy days or periods in life, and these factors would all affect our responses to researchers and therefore the validity of their data.

Argyle's work on satisfaction in marriage is supported by a large number of studies, for instance Cramer (1995) found that unmarried, divorced or widowed people in their 20s and 30s have a much higher risk of dying than their married peers. Gove (1979) and Bee (1998) have shown that both mental and physical health are better in married than single people. However, Argyle and Henderson (1985) point out that the quality of the married relationship was a determining factor in how beneficial the marriage is. An unhappy, miserable marriage is unlikely to lead to increased health, mental or physical.

Marriage as a life event

Living closely with another person, whether as a married couple or as cohabitees, involves great adjustments and, almost certainly, a time of increased stress until the readjustments are accepted. This is perhaps why marriage scored highly on Holmes and Rahe's SRRS. Even if people have shared a flat or house with others, they will almost certainly have had their own personal space, such as their own bedroom. When couples live together as a unit they are likely not to have this, their own personal space, and that can be a difficult thing to adjust to. Humans too have to establish a pecking order, even if it is to do with responsibilities in the kitchen, say! However much we promote the ideal of equality within a relationship, almost all of us show a need to have a known place in our social or other order. We also adapt our self-image to circumstances and need to adapt to our new image as part of a couple instead of a girl- or boy-friend or fiancé(e). So self-acceptance as well as dominance are two areas in which a couple have to make significant adjustments. This is probably as true today as it was in the 1960s, even though some of the adjustments may be slightly different.

Adjustments also need to be made throughout the marriage, of course. Couples report that in the early years they spend a lot of time together, interact a lot, talk and share recreational time together a great deal, as well as arguing and making up! Having children to care for means that the couple are not able to spend so much time together, whether on their own as a two-some or being together for social activities. Then as they age they are once more able to be a couple together for most of their shared time, and many people reported this was a satisfying adjustment to have made (Swenson, Eskew and Kolheff 1981).

Duval (1971) suggested a model of adulthood called the family life cycle, which suggested that initially marriage had a 'honeymoon period' recalled by people as the most happy in spite of the readjustments which they have to make when they share real and emotional space with their loved other. The amount of time spent in this period would vary from couple to couple, typically ending with the birth of the first child.

Evaluation of Duval's model

This model falls down as it is both biased to the traditional western marriage, and does not look at the variety of marriages we have today. Second marriages, for instance, are ignored. Most marriages also do not exist in a family vacuum! The young couples' parents are likely to be closely involved in the first stages, providing various kinds of support and encouragement. However, a good point of this model is the way it shows marriage as a dynamic relationship and not a fixed one.

Summary of marriage and partnering research

- Five types of marriage were identified by Cuber and Harroff in the 1960s; and in the 1970s Duberman produced a different set of three marriage types.
- Problems with both these classifications include the time context of the studies and the research methods used.
- Marriage is a social arrangement and social factors and norms are dynamic and vary, so research findings will also vary with time.
- Much of the research has been based on interviews and questionnaires and self-reporting which have possible bias, reliability and validity problems of their own.
- The gender difference in satisfaction in marriage could be explained by men having, outside marriage, a much poorer social network for support than women have.

- This difference could also be caused by males wanting to be cared for or needing a partner as a status symbol, more than females do; or by women feeling more able to voice concerns about their marriages compared to men.
- A particular difficulty in researching marriage is that different cultures have different ideas on what is important in a satisfying marriage, and how important the various factors are. There are also differences in how marriage is seen, for instance whether it is a romantic-based bond or a socially-based one.
- Research such as Argyle's supports the concept that marriage increases happiness and contentment, especially for men.
- Research also showed that satisfaction in marriage is high at the beginning, then dips, and then rises again forming a U-shaped curve. But this has been shown to be a western structure and is not supported by research in other cultures.
- Today as social behaviours have changed, research focuses on partnerships as well as on marriages.
- Recent research supports older findings that being in a marriage/partnership increases physical and mental health and lifespan compared to unmarried, divorced or widowed people.
- Marriage is quite high on the SRRS stress score, and this may be because of the adjustments that most people have to make when marrying, e.g. adjustments to personal space, self-image and dominance. This pattern of adjustment has been used in the Family Life Cycle model, though this is clearly based only on traditional western marriages.

Parenthood

Erikson (1968) thought of parenthood as the resolution of part of the generativity crisis, as having a child can mean the opportunity to care for or nurture another person as well as making a contribution to the future. He saw parenthood as part of the developmental process, especially for women. In his model, discussed in Chapter 2, a woman needs to develop her 'productive inner space' if she is to be truly fulfilled, and being a parent is one sure way to this fulfilment.

Holmes and Rahe's SRRS ranked becoming a parent (or gaining a new member of the family) as fourteenth in the list of stressful life events. Certainly many parents, especially new parents, are surprised by the changes that having a family brings. Galinsky (1981) suggests that most people don't actually realise how much their lives will change once they have a baby, and the tiredness and the disruption of the adults' routines is a probable cause of pre-baby times being seen as idyllic, even though most of the couples interviewed said the baby was wanted and regarded as delightful.

Progress exercise

How do you think life changes for new parents? What are the costs or stressors involved, and what are the rewards or uplifts? How might working and social life be affected?

Since 90 per cent of adults do become parents (Bee 1994), it seems people view the rewards of parenthood as worth the stressors! Of course, this could be the effect of a social norm, the positive expectation and approval of having a child. On the other hand, many people also say that the desire for a child is an innate drive, nothing to do with social norms or society's views or one's own overt beliefs. This certainly might help to explain the very great lengths some couples are prepared to go to in order to have a family.

Types of parenting

Much of the research on parenthood has been done in western culture, so care needs to be taken in generalising to people worldwide. Parenthood may be a planned state, or unplanned; it may be welcomed or unwanted; it can occur within or outside marriage; it can be the result of many different motivations.

Gender differences in parenting

In western and several other cultures parenting seems to have been seen as a female task rather than a male task. This is possibly because of the biological aspects of motherhood, but the assumption that parenting is more a 'woman thing' than a 'couple thing' now seems to be at odds with modern thought, though not perhaps with everyday reality. Within this general idea there are some different psychological views; Mead's highly personal opinion, the psychodynamic approach, the humanistic approach and the modern western model.

First is Mead's (1949) pronouncement that fathers are a 'biological necessity but a social accident'! Not many people today would support this idea because it seems so prejudiced, very gender-biased, and disrespectful of the many fathers who are responsible partners and parents.

Second is psychodynamic theory, and Benedek (1959) points out the possible link between a girl's early identification with her mother and the later development of her own maternal instinct. In this way she could re-experience the pleasures and pains of her own early years as she cares for her own child. Alternatively, psychodynamic theory could also suggest that by caring for her infant the woman could heal her own 'inner child' of any traumatic or unhappy memories from early childhood. This does not explain why a man might not need to experience just those same things, however, and like almost all psychodynamic theory the problem is the difficulty or impossibility of obtaining any empirical evidence either for or against its suggestions.

Third is the Humanistic approach, suggesting that we progress, individually, through life and make our way up through a series or hierarchy of needs (Maslow 1968). Central among these needs are love and belonging. A close adult relationship and a family to care for would dovetail with these two main needs, and this approach offers an alternative view of marriage/partnerships and parenting. It suggests that we have a drive for love and belonging which can be fulfilled in a close emotional relationship and in being parents. This explanation can explain the powerful drive many adults experience to become parents, but as with the psychodynamic approach empirical evidence is lacking.

In some parts of modern western society there is a fourth view regarding the male parent's role. This role seems to have increased as it is now often the norm for a father to be present at his child's birth so he can be involved from the beginning. Lugo and Hershey (1979) suggested that careful preparation for and better understanding of the male and female parental roles would improve the experience of parenting. Very recently a few birth units in the UK have developed this idea, introducing double rooms in their obstetric units so both the father and the mother can care for the new baby together from the first hours. The aim of this is that the new or increased family group should include rather than exclude the father, making the parents more equal in their relationships with each other and the new baby. This may also affect the father–baby attachment bonding positively, but of course this arrangement will depend on the personal feelings of the parents. Such projects also stem from suggestions such as Dinnerstein's (1976) that attitudes towards parenting would change if men could take more share in it

Cultural differences in parenting

The western-culture approach to this life stage necessarily limits the usefulness of much research. The **time context** is another limitation as so many studies have assumed the mid-twentieth-century western culture as the main pattern for parenthood.

This does not allow for many modern western cultural patterns, nor for those from non-western cultures. For instance, government statistics show that an increasing proportion of children are born outside marriage, and many have made the assumption that these children are being brought up in single-parent families. This is not necessarily at all true. In our own culture many couples live together, have a commitment to each other and to their children, and cohabit with no formal marriage. They may have had alternative ceremonies, such as Wiccan (pagan) or Partnership ones which are not usually recognised by law; or they may have what was formerly known as 'an understanding'. Birth records in the UK show the large majority of births being registered by both parents, most sharing a home address (Social Trends 1999), and this supports the idea that the social norms of parenthood in our modern culture have changed.

Another cultural change in parenthood is shown by the increasing number of lesbian and gay couples who are also becoming parents by artificial insemination/surrogacy. Though one would expect same-sex partners to have similar parenthood experiences to those of heterosexual couples, some differences have been found. In a small sample, gay fathers were shown as being stricter but more responsive towards their children, and they took more care in the child's social-isation than heterosexual fathers (Bigner and Jacobsen 1989). But the sample bias, the result of the small sample size and low frequency of the target population, means we cannot assume the conclusions are generalisable to the gay population. A similar comparative study on lesbian and heterosexual couples and their children used several assessment measures and found that though both groups showed similar adjustments to being a couple, i.e. to marriage or similar state, the lesbian couples were more aware than the heterosexual group of the skills needed as a parent. The same criticisms apply to this study as to the Bigner and Jacobsen one, above. However, the American Psychological Association (2006) states that studies of same-sex couples as parents show no differences in their children's development compared to children of heterosexual couples.

One well-known cultural difference between much of modern western society, an individualist culture, and collectivist cultures is isolation. Many new parents in our own culture do not live with or even near their own parents, the grandparents, and therefore cannot call on them for help and support, whereas in collectivist cultures there would be that extended family support to help care for the child and reduce parental stress. For example, the !Kung in the Kalahari always have family around, and young babies are actually carried by one or other family member for all twenty-four hours of the day.

Effects of parenting on the individual

'Two's company, three's a crowd' is a common saying and belief and it is often true! But when it comes to starting a family this concept is not helpful. It is common sense as well as a research conclusion that when a couple have a young child they will have much less time and attention for each other (Bee 1994). Especially if there is little support available from the traditional extended family, the couple will spend less time together, whether for chatting and sharing experiences and ideas, or sexually. Traditionally, but less frequently today, becoming a parent has been associated with the early years of adulthood and the early years of a marriage. This means that the couple would not have had a great deal of time to mature separately as well as in their relationship, and they would also be unlikely to be financially so comfortable. This would make the parenting life event, adjusting to parenthood, more difficult, especially if the couple are under pressure to become established in their careers.

Generally speaking, research studies show that happiness in their relationship or marriage once the couple become parents is greatest if they are young and well-off financially (Bee 1994). For most parents though, the birth of the first child reduces general satisfaction (Reibstein and Richards 1992) and Eysenck (1990) has shown this occurs in a very wide range of cultures and religious groups and is independent of the level of education the parents have. In the past this drop in satisfaction has been greater in women than in men (Ruble *et al*. 1988), doubtless because the financial and especially social constraints of a young baby or child most affect the mother at home.

Interestingly, it has been suggested that for many adults the birth of the first child ranks sixth out of 102 on these people's personal stressful life-events scale. None of this means parents are dissatisfied with their new status and responsibilities, nor that the baby or child is unwelcome. After all, we humans are well used to having mixed up feelings! Most parents also admit to being delighted at having their baby, and report that they feel the positive aspects of having the child outweigh the negative ones. These views could be interpreted as support for Turner and Helms' (1989) theory that parenthood gives:

- A sense of purpose, and responsibility
- A sense of achievement, in Erikson's terms the successful resolution of the generativity versus stagnation conflict
- Fulfilment of what the person's culture expects of them
- Control and authority over one's dependants
- Legitimate exchange of love and affection
- Increased personal happiness and stability through the new, stable family unit.

This theory is very useful as it can explain, at least partially, why some people are prepared to go to great lengths with, for example, IVF or adoption to become parents. Their motivation could be an innate drive, a social drive, or could be based on the six ideas listed above.

Commentary on parenting research

Much of the research into parenthood as a life event is relatively old, and should be seen in its time context. It is also mainly related to western-industrialised society in the background culture and outlook, and this bias too needs to be acknowledged. Within these limits then it gives a picture of parenthood in a type of society in the mid- and late-twentieth century. This clear identification of the target population shows the importance of locating in culture and time the social and cultural norms affecting people and parenthood, so we need to be wary of applying what was learned about parenthood then to society and cultures existing now.

In many western cultures it is increasingly the norm for both parents to continue with paid work after the birth of children; financial pressures might therefore not be as great but other pressures take their place. Many modern parents worry about not being at home with their young children, and discussions about this stressful and emotive topic fill all sorts of magazines and newspapers.

What new pressures would you suggest new parents feel, if they are financially comfortable as both of them are continuing to work outside the home?

And what reason(s) can you come up with for many young couples delaying parenthood to their 30s or older?

Progress exercise

Delayed parenthood

It is also true that in our own culture couples are not just marrying later but also waiting till their later 20s, 30s or their 40s to become parents. It is suggested that the move towards delaying parenthood until the 30s is a trend, not a 'blip' in society, and the causes include the knock-on effect of student gap years, the increase in four-year degree courses, and women wanting to build their careers before taking a motherhood break. This new society has been depicted very success-fully by various books and films which show the conflict between career, independence and the biological clock's ticking. And a small but possibly increasing number of today's young women are choos-ing not to become parents at all (Jones 1995). In 1980 only 1 in 10 women aged 40 were childless, whereas in 2002 the number has risen to 1 in 5.

Another point worth making is that people and therefore their relationships vary, and a pattern is not the same as a rule. Cox *et al.* (1999) showed in a review of relevant literature that the quality of a couple's own relationship, their skills in communicating with each other and resolving conflicts, their own upbringing and the man's feelings about becoming a father were all significant variables in how couples feel as parents. This means that individual differences between couples is another factor in the experience of parenthood; not just their separate and individual psychosocial histories but vital skills such as communication will vary and affect the relationship.

Empty nest or crowded nest?

Many parents feel a great increase in satisfaction when their children are grown and ready to join the adult world. This may be because of a sense of a job well done; the baby has been cared for, the child has been prepared for its adult life. Or it may be anticipation of the child flying the nest, leaving home to make her or his own way in life! Certainly the 'empty-nest syndrome', where one or both parents feel almost bereaved when their child moves on into adulthood and leaves home, is not experienced by all couples. There are individuals who do, deeply, miss their child or children and see their going as the end of the most important and enjoyable phase of their own life. But research shows that many people have the opposite experience. A large number of couples admit to relishing the rediscovery of their own freedom, each other, and other resources for themselves again (Bee 1994). This is enhanced if it is combined with feelings of pleasure and satisfaction in how the child or children have turned out.

In the last few years another scenario has started to become more well-known, that is the 'crowded nest'. This is where the adult child does not leave or returns to their family home and cohabits as an adult with their parents. Such adults have been termed 'boomerang' children, and a survey of over one thousand people aged 16 to 64 by BT Openworld (in *The Times* 21 March 2002) found that 27 per cent of young adults return home to live with their parents at least once, 10 per cent returning four times before they are finally independent. Of these adults 40 per cent still return home more than once a week for creature comforts, and 10 per cent of 35–44-year-olds still take their washing home. This may be the reason why 43 per cent of the parents do not develop a close adult relationship with their adult children until they have finally left the family home. The reasons given for this increase in returning home to live seem to be mainly financial, and York University's Centre for Housing Policy also identifies other specific non-psychological factors including high house prices, student debt, and the shrinkage of numbers of young adults in full-time employment.

A different and psychological interpretation of the crowded nest is really a **socio-biological** one. In our society today we have a much lengthened lifespan. Biologically we are designed to wear out and die after only a few decades, but this span is doubled and may lengthen more. A possible effect of this is a corresponding lengthening of pre-adulthood and young adulthood. It has been suggested that the antics of people in their twenties and even thirties are in fact a 'new adolescence' and that people are not maturing and becoming responsible adults until their mid-30s (Richardson 2001). Richardson also cites the high cost of housing and the importance of consumer goods as reasons for younger adults to stay with their parents and postpone adulthood. The research tracked nearly 200 young adults over five years, and the results are supported by research from Bath University. It is also suggested that continuing education into the adult years puts off financial and therefore traditional adult independence (in Harlow 2001). These changes have, however, been recognised by retailers such as supermarkets who target different age-groups in different ways, and even by George W. Bush, the American President, who seems to consider his pre-aged 40 drink-driving conviction as a 'youthful indiscretion'.

There may be an underlying socio-biological perspective to some of the more recent changes in parenthood. It seems we are descended from populations who had a far shorter lifespan than we now enjoy. Our life expectancy is more than double that of our hunter-gatherer ancestors and even our ancestors of a few centuries ago, and so it has been suggested that the stages in life, from childhood to adolescence, early then middle and older adulthood, all are now greatly lengthening. So our **hunter-gatherer ancestors** living 100,000 years ago would have become parents probably in their teens, and grandparents in their 30s. It is assumed that death would have come to most before they reached age 50. But in only the last century human lifespan has generally increased so much that the stages of adolescence, early, middle and late adulthood now last much longer. This could mean that a psychological change of attitude about life stages and expectancy has also come about, leading to new adjustments from both parents and their adult children. This is because the extended lifespan gives a much longer learning period and thus we can develop our intelligence and skills to a higher level which, obviously, is adaptive as it enables us to become more successful.

Summary of parenting research

- Becoming a parent is a very obvious life change, and Erikson thought this change was a very significant contribution to generativity.
- Almost all parents report delight in the new child and consider this pleasure outweighs the negative aspects of parenthood.
- Many cultures, including western culture, traditionally regard parenting more as a female than a male role or task. Psychodynamic theory would support this as based on the woman's identification with her own mother when a young girl.
- There is evidence that the male role in parenting, fatherhood, is increasing in some parts of western society.
- Research into parenting also includes one-parent and gay parent families. But methodological problems have arisen, for instance the very small and therefore non-representative samples of gay parents, and the false assumption of some research that an unmarried mother or father is a one-parent family.
- Significant adjustments to parenthood are made as it is a major life change. The loss of sleep and extra work involved may be a main cause of the drop in satisfaction with the marriage, but this may be a western cultural effect as in cultures where the extended family helps the new parents such a drop is not seen.
- A problem with the research into this area is that so much is old, and that it is possible for social changes to have altered factors such as parental expectations and adjustments, age of becoming a parent, and both parents returning to work.
- Individual differences between couples are likely to be considerable, such as their communication skills or psychosocial histories, and this too could affect the experience of parenthood.

- When children become adult some parents feel grief that a fulfilling time is over, but others feel a sense of satisfaction in a life stage completed, and increased pleasure in their own relationship.
- A recent development in western culture has been the return of the adult children to the parental home, usually for economic reasons, which can cause stress and reduce parental satisfaction.

Divorce

This is the most stressful life event apart from the death of one's spouse, according to Holmes and Rahe, and yet about 40 per cent of marriages in the UK end in divorce and in the USA an even greater percentage do. So this stressful life event is a common behaviour. It has been suggested that some personalities are more likely to divorce, that there might be some innate traits which make divorce more likely. Plomin (1997) found a higher concordance rate for divorce in monozygotic (MZ or identical) twins than for dizygotic (DZ or non-identical) twins, which could mean that there is a genetic input. This could be an inherited predisposition to unhappiness, or any other trait which would make a person less easy to live with. There is certainly some belief, unsubstantiated, that people choose the same sort of partner time and again, and this could be because they are genetically predisposed to being attracted to a certain type. If this were true then perhaps genetic traits might contribute to the likelihood of divorce or even serial divorces, for instance if the person concerned was only attracted to a particular age-range or physical type.

Changing divorce rate

A different slant on divorce is that the high level of divorces today compared to fifty years ago could be caused at least partially by the ease with which couples can now start but also end formal relationships, which was not always true in our own culture. The key factor here might be that people have both higher and less realistic ideas and expectations of marriage and rush into this idealised state – and then when it does not live up to their hopes they are quick to abandon it (Durkin 1995). This could be backed up by Levinson's (1978) theory because, if both partners expect their marriage to fulfil their Dream, and yet this does not happen, for instance if only one Dream is being realised, then the marriage might break down. The high level of divorce among couples both of whom are married for the first time could be said to support this idea. In 2000, 70 per cent of divorces were from such marriages.

Timing of divorce

Divorce is more likely to happen during certain times in a marriage, that is during the first five years, and after fifteen to twenty-five years (Turnbull 1995). This doesn't support the common idea of the so-called seven-year itch!

Divorce and health

What divorce actually means to people varies a great deal. It certainly affects people's physical and mental health, which ties in with the stress experienced. Divorced people are much more likely to suffer from mental problems, and their overall health is worse than that of unmarried or widowed people. But there are exceptions. Buunk (1996) identified several factors which made divorcing people less likely to have health difficulties, as follows:

* A more distant relationship with their former partner
* Taking the initiative to end the marriage/relationship
* Having strong social network(s)
* In another intimate and satisfying relationship
* Having high self-esteem
* Being independent
* Tolerating change well
* Having an egalitarian sex-role attitude (choosing equality).

All the above help to make the divorce experience less stressful and easier to cope with, but common sense would say that it is unlikely-to-impossible that both of a divorcing pair should have all the above advantageous factors. It is also possible that the stress and stress-related health problems might be the cause, and not the effect, of the relationship break-up.

Subsequent marriages/partnerships

Divorced people are unlikely to stay on their own. In our culture the majority of divorcees either remarry or cohabit, which shows that in the modern world marriage and partnership are different states compared to a generation ago because of changing social norms, and many families now are step-families. Studying divorce is really complicated as many remarriages also end in divorce, more so in the USA than in the UK. Serial marriages are the norm in some parts of American society, where the divorce rate in subsequent marriages is even higher than the 45 per cent in first marriages (Gross 2001).

In the UK there has been a recent reduction in the divorce rate, particularly in divorces from the first marriage. In 2000 the rate was the lowest for 22 years, at 141,135 divorces. The percentage of married people divorcing in that year is 1.27, or 12.7 per 1000, and the highest proportion of these comes from the 25- to 29-year-old age-group. This would tie in with Erikson's suggested crisis, where intimacy had been tried for but not achieved, so for these younger adults they were, from his theory, back in isolation again. The average age for divorce is older, tying in with the data suggesting a later 'risk' period; for men it is age 41.3 years and for women 38.3.

A spokesperson for Relate quoted by PA News for AOL (2001) suggests that the overall downward trend in the divorce rate is mainly caused by people choosing to wait and marry later rather than sooner in life. Perhaps the greater emotional maturity and sense of what they really want from the relationship is due in part to resolving the intimacy versus isolation crisis, and also having a better idea of what they want from life, plus seeing the effects of divorce on their parents and their own generations.

Progress exercise

What factors can you think of which would explain that though the greatest percentage of people divorcing are under 30 years old, the average age for divorce is around 40 years old?

Divorce and the family

It should also be remembered that for most people involved divorce is a sad event. It usually means the end of hopes for the marriage and for the planned future, and there may be real grief, feelings of real bereavement, especially if a family is also being broken up. One factor which seems to be powerful in the effects of divorce on the family, i.e. the children, is how much conflict there was around the separation. When young adults were asked about their feeling on their parents' divorce, those from high-conflict families said they coped better if their parents did not stay together but divorced. However, those from low-conflict families coped better if the parents did not divorce but instead stayed together.

Finally, we should all remember that divorce is a very sensitive area indeed, and researching such a socially sensitive event is not easy, from the ethical point of view particularly.

Stages of divorce

No life event just happens, out of the blue. There is always a progression, however short, and several psychologists have tried to identify such a progression for divorce. One such model which ties in with both common sense and anecdotal comments is Bohannon's (1970). This suggests a progression of six stages culminating in the divorced couple coming to terms with their new life apart.

All stage theories can be criticised for being prescriptive and assuming that all people behave in the same way, they all ignore individual differences. And it seems likely that, though the above stages make good sense and so have surface validity, the actual order in which a divorcing couple go through the stages, and how many of the stages they complete, has to vary. And we may know of someone who is divorced but sadly hasn't been able to make the psychological separation of stage 6, and is still looking backwards.

Gender differences in divorce

Research shows that in general women find it harder to cope with divorce than men do. This is because usually women lose out more financially and also have to cope with a greater parental role and

Table 3.2 Bohannon's model of six stages of divorce	
Stage	Description
1. The emotional divorce	The relationship, the marriage or partnership, develops conflicts and disintegrates psychologically, with recriminations
2. The legal divorce	The marriage is ended by the courts by going through the legal procedures necessary. The divorce is official
3. The economic divorce	The couple's various assets are divided up as approved, if necessary, legally
4. The co-parental divorce	If there are any children of the marriage then issues of custody, access and support are decided
5. The community divorce	Relationships with family and friends alter as necessary to accommodate the couple becoming separate
6. Psychic divorce	The two divorced people adapt and adjust separately to their new state and status

Source: After Bohannon 1970

responsibility (Rutter and Rutter 1992). Gross (2001) states that after divorce 84 per cent of children live with their mothers, usually in single-parent families. On the other hand, though each partner finds divorce highly stressful it is men who are more adversely affected by this divorce stress than women. This could be because most men have weak support networks outside their work, perhaps even within work, and this may also be a reason why they tend not to initiate actual divorce proceedings (Gross 1996), as well as because of lack of access to children, increased money problems and having to move out of the family home.

Divorced women, even though the majority of them too make a second committed relationship, could have benefits from ending their marriage. Cooper (1996) cites Woollett and Fuller as showing that many divorced mothers gain a valuable sense of achievement and empowerment following the divorce, as they learn they can manage their lives successfully. But Cooper also cites Lewis' comments that these opinions may be flawed evidence as the women could be comparing how they feel in the present with the unhappy experiences just before and during their divorces.

Cultural differences in divorce

Plenty of evidence shows that there are cultural differences in the timing and frequency of divorce, as well as attitudes to divorce.

Most of the research data are based on western, industrialised society, but even here there are cultural variations. Hetherington and Stanley-Hagan (1999) report that, in the USA, more non-Hispanic white people marry than African-Americans, and the marriages take place when younger. The African-Americans are also more likely to end their marriages, with or without formal divorces, and less likely to remarry. This could reflect different cultural attitudes to both marriage and divorce.

Some religious cultures, such as Roman Catholicism, do not recognise divorce as the bond made between the couple is believed to be sanctioned by God and it is therefore not possible for it to be undone by mere humans. This of course can mean that the marriage still legally exists, but in fact may also mean that separations and subsequent partnerships still occur. There may be far greater psychological traumas and negative emotions such as guilt for the person moving out of the marriage. This would be an example of where the stage theory of divorce, outlined earlier, still applies as the marriage is ended in fact, even if not in law.

Other religious cultures seem to make it extremely easy to divorce, at least from the male's point of view. In spite of the Q'ran's strong support of women and of the family, some Muslim cultures recognise divorce if the husband just says three times that he divorces his wife. She can have no option but to acquiesce to this.

Other religion-based cultures may be more supportive of relation-ship breakdowns. Israeli kibbutzim have a strong collectivist culture where the good of the community is most important. Life is organised for the benefit of the group, and so it is not really surprising that data shows less stress and easier adjustments following divorce than in our society (Kaffman 1993). This seems to be because the way life is organised means that there were few sources of conflict between the former couple, even though the emotional trauma of a failed relationship is as difficult for them as for any other couple.

Divorce and its effects and difficulties are, however, a part of life in most cultures, as illustrated by the job description of court justices in Zambia. Section 1.0 lists one of their duties as the hearing and determination of cases involving the refusal by some husbands to share household property with divorced wives.

Can you think why it has been suggested that older women feel they are less likely than older men to find a new relationship or marriage after divorce? Is there any actual evidence for your idea?

Progress exercise

Effects of divorce on the individual

The adjustments to divorce are mainly described above. There are the adjustments to the stress of the event, and to the conflicts and negative emotions likely to be involved. The emotions are difficult to adjust to as they are powerful and unpleasant. Nobody likes to feel they have failed, however much they may blame the other party. And this other person is likely to have been someone they once loved, with happy memories now buried. There may be internally conflicting emotions too; grief and relief, pain of loss and gain of freedom beckoning, disappointment and excitement. These things often lead to problems at work, as people find it harder to concentrate, and there is the increased likelihood of physical and mental health problems too. All these are signs of difficulty in adjusting to this life event. Research into increased health risks and abnormal behaviours also shows increased incidence of violence, suicide, and homicide as well as the reduced immunity (Gottman 1998).

Strong negative effects often seem to come during the actual divorce process, the formalising of the relationship breakdown. This is almost certainly because the legal proceedings bring home the actuality of the break-up, the virtual impossibility of the relationship returning to a former, happy state. The degree of difficulty in adjusting seems to depend on five main factors. These are:

1. How long the couple have been married. Clearly, the longer a marriage has lasted the more difficult it will be to let go, and the more shared friends they will have to renegotiate friendships with, the more goods they will have gathered together, and the more history they will have in common.
2. How old the couple are. Younger people may feel they have more time ahead in which to make a new and better relationship; conversely, older people, both men and women, may feel time is running out for them (Berk 1998).
3. How many and how old any children are. Most people in a divorce will be concerned for their children's well-being; aware they may suffer emotionally from the divorce; worried if the children are not yet adults as to how it might affect their future, as research shows that school-age children take time to adapt to their parents' divorce on the whole, and may be more anti-social for a time, especially boys (Berk 1998).
4. Whose idea the divorce was. A person who decides they need to divorce will adapt and adjust differently, quicker maybe, than a person who did not seek the divorce in the first place.
5. How the divorce process was perceived. The actuality of the divorce process may be more of a trauma to some than to others. If they feel or accept blame then this may make the process harder to accept, and the public nature of the process may also make adjusting more difficult.

The year following the divorce is difficult for both parties, male and female. Most of them report disorganisation, plus a drop in income. This latter is worse for the woman if her role had been as home-maker and she had no career outside her home or had taken a career break and is therefore out of touch or out of date in her skills. Research does support this concept, as employed women who divorce have better self-esteem than unemployed divorcing women (Bisagni and Eckenrode 1995). A different explanation for this would be that a person at work has a wider and more varied circle of acquaintances and friends than someone unemployed.

What other reasons can you think of to explain why an employed person might adjust to divorce more easily than an unemployed person, whether male or female?

Progress exercise

Summary of divorce

- Divorce is a major, stressful life event, ending about 40 per cent of marriages in the UK.
- There is evidence of a genetic component to this behaviour; but the ease of starting and ending formal relationships could be another important factor.
- Unrealistic ideas and expectations of marriage could also be one cause, and this could fit in with Levinson's theory. If the two Dreams of the couple are not compatible, or if they are mutually exclusive, then the marriage is less likely to last.
- The high rate of divorces from first marriages and also during the first five years seem to support this idea, and also Erikson's intimacy/isolation crisis with the attempt at intimacy failing. The other peak in divorces, after between fifteen and twenty-five years of marriage could also fit Levinson's, but not Erikson's, theory if the people involved see that even after all this time their Dream is still not fulfilled, then they end the marriage while they still have time to pursue their own Dream.
- Divorced people in general are not as satisfied nor as healthy as married people, but they are likely to remarry.
- The amount of conflict around the divorce has an effect on children of the marriage.

- Bohannon's stage theory of divorce suggests a progression through six stages starting with the psychological disintegration of the relationship and ending with the psychic separation and adjustment to the new, single state.
- Research shows that women find it harder to adjust to divorce than men do, but men are more adversely affected by the divorce. The majority remarry another partner.
- There is a range of cultural differences in divorce and remarriage, including religion-based differences.
- The effects of divorce seem worst during the actual divorce process, and depend on five factors including the age of the people concerned and how many and how old any children are.
- Another psychological factor in the effects of divorce is likely to be the amount of social support each person has access to, as this is such a stressful life event.

Further reading

Karp, H. (2002) *The Happiest Baby*. London: Michael Joseph/Penguin.

Marland, F. (2002) From China with love, in *The Times*, 4 May is a detailed and very human account of the efforts made to adopt a child from abroad, with a happy ending.

Santrock, J.W. (1992) *A Topical Approach to Life-Span Development*, 4th edn, New York: McGraw-Hill Humanities has excellent chapters on social development in early and middle adulthood.

www.psychology.org/links/Environment_Behavior_Relationships/Marriage/ contains useful links to both marriage and divorce.

www.responsiblefatherhood.org. This is the site of the IRFFR, an American, non-profit organisation dedicated to empowering and supporting fathers to become actively involved in the lives of their children.

Late Adulthood

> One would know the first cold breath of old age . . . when one
> found oneself in a world where there was no-one left to whom
> one was a child.
>
> (E. Goudge 1940)

Late adulthood: introduction

As with the terms 'early' and 'middle', 'late' adulthood is largely
a matter of opinion! When one is 17, being 30 seems not only tre-
mendously far off but impossible to imagine and also very old. Age
40 is really, really old and age 50 is ancient. But from other age
perspectives the labels differ. To a 50-year-old being 20 or even 30
seems rather young! So we have first to try and define what we
mean, psychologically, by late adulthood; in much psychological
writing this seems to be the 60s and the decades following to most
researchers in this field.

What does being old mean to you?
When do people become old, at what age or other factor?

A problem with researching late adulthood is the very negative social perception of ageing in our culture. Many younger people find the idea of growing old frightening and/or revolting. The workplace usually discriminates against older adults, sometimes because more experienced and senior people cost more, sometimes because of what seems like pure bias. This attitude is slowly being redressed as some organisations find that older people can be more reliable or better at dealing with others, and in the UK legislation has been passed to end discrimination because of age, legally. However it is true that for many adults ageing will bring a degree of physical and even mental decline, sometimes a great deal, and this can cause a lot of distress. This may be the reason behind **ageism**; or it may be that once people retire there is a strange mix of feelings from younger people. There could be envy because the old do not have to go to work, but have pensions and are perceived as having more freedom – but also that as non-workers they are not contributing to the community any more and so are no longer important. If we are honest, most of us do have a stereotype of what being aged/old is like. Perhaps your answers to the questions above give a clue as to your own stereotype of the old. Does this fit all old people, and do you know, or know of, any old people who don't actually fit your answers? Probably 'no' to the former, and 'yes' to the latter, are likely to be your responses!

Older adults and culture

As in previous chapters we need to remember that in our own, western industrialised culture youth and youthfulness are prized. People who cannot claim to be young are prepared to go to great lengths to appear young and to have 'young' beliefs and attitudes. Products which are not new are reinvented by the manufacturers or advertisers to change in order to become new – with the exception of a few traditional products such as Coca-Cola® – and even that is sometimes referred to as *classic*, to make sure we all realise this fact and do not think it is merely old! Even those of us who actually are young adults are caught up, and spend time and money to keep looking and acting young.

Progress exercise

What evidence can you think of to support the above ideas that people are prepared to spend time and money, to go to great lengths, to preserve or imitate youthfulness?

This attitude or mindset is not usually shown in collectivist cultures. Here a person is valued for their contribution to the community or family group, and older adults are valued for their accumulated wisdom, knowledge and experience. In traditional Chinese culture the most important members of the social group or family were the elderly, the grandmothers and grandfathers. This belief in the wisdom of age might be a reason why until quite recently the rulers of such cultures were rather older than the presidents or prime ministers of western countries. But this is a culture thing, and in our own culture we read of our history and the control of local communities by the village elders – the term is still used to mean the people in control, the rulers, though these people do not actually have to be older adults.

Social theories of late adulthood development

According to Levinson (1978) there is a late adult transition between 60 and 65 years. This is a time when people realise they are declining physically and that their own community and culture is now regarding them as 'old'. We might interpret this as the start of coming to terms with one's own mortality, starting to accept that one is growing old and can no longer do everything one did as a 20- or 30-year-old. Of course, there are exceptions to this – examples are often from the media world as we notice them more and their self-publicity seems part of their life. But for most of us, the signs of ageing cannot be delayed indefinitely.

Erikson's theory

Erikson had late adulthood as his eighth and last 'age of man' (1980). He suggested that this stage started early, in the 40s, and said that the crisis belonging to this final life stage was of ego integrity versus despair. What he meant was that people in this stage of life need to make some sense of their own life, their personal history. If they can integrate the outcomes of the previous stages, i.e. feel that in some way their life has had meaning, has been worthwhile, they progress and gain wisdom, and retain their personal integrity. If they cannot do this they are then full of despair as their existence has been meaningless, a waste of time. This idea has some appeal, some face validity. No one would want to feel their life has been pointless; to themselves and to others, to humanity. But as has been said before in previous chapters, the non-empirical research data and the psychodynamic assumptions behind this theory weaken the power of his model.

Levinson's theory

A discussion of Levinson's theory in early and middle adulthood can be found in Chapters 2 and 3.

Following these stages he suggests a late adult transition into the final stage of Late Adulthood, from age 65 to the end of life. Levinson felt that this stage should involve the acceptance that life has an end; that we cannot control this ending; that if people are to be happy they need to accept and live with the fact that life is coming to an end sooner rather than later, that they can accept whatever life has been like, and that they need to be realistic about what can be achieved from now on. This is a very demanding theory and stage, and illustrates an ideal. This part of his stage theory also illustrates the change in cultural norms of the western world since he wrote. In many parts of current western culture dying and death are the modern taboos, things which are not spoken of nor openly acknowledged, and because of this have become events which people find difficult to speak of. It can almost seem that death is embarrassing, even offensive, not a natural process, which attitude really contradicts much of Levinson's ideas of this stage.

Burnside's decade approach

This was suggested by Burnside *et al.* (1979) and Craig (1992). Its great advantage is that it at once makes clear that we cannot group all older adults together as one cohort. Older adults are a diverse group, not just in year-age but also in ability, life events, attitude and so on. This of course means that people will both experience and adjust differently to growing older.

Obviously the decade demarcations are only a guide, as individual differences will apply and this theory is, like almost all theories, a generalisation. But though each person may experience a varying number of the suggested events and transitions and a varying degree of health and other adjustments, this pattern is a useful one. This model originally stopped at age 99, but in today's world there is an increasing number of people living beyond their century. Extra factors which might affect an individual's pattern or adjustment to old age could be the degree of economic independence and social support s/he has. You may know from your previous studies that social support is a vital factor in coping with stress, and many of the changes of old age are stressful. No one welcomes health, cognitive or other problems! As friends die an older person can start to feel very alone and very isolated, especially if they have few if any peers with whom to talk over shared memories. Economic factors can also be stress factors, and we have all read of older people's fears in winter time over the cost of keeping warm. If becoming older also involves being less able to be financially independent then there may be a variety of stressors such as the older person's fears as to how they can cope, or whether their family will help, or whether the family will resent such help.

Social disengagement theory (Cummings and Henry 1961)

This theory was regarded as the first real attempt to relate ageing to people's social situation or community.

The theory states that there is mutual withdrawal in old age – of the ageing adult from her/his community and society, and also vice versa, i.e. of the community and society from the ageing adult. This withdrawal involves compulsory retirement; death of peers, perhaps of a spouse or partner or close friend(s); children moving away from the area and continuing building their own careers and families, and

Table 4.1 Burnside's decade approach to growing older

Stage	Decade (years)	Description
The 'young' old	60–69	This is the great transition period where older adults have to make efforts to adapt to their losses and gains. Peers such as friends and colleagues are getting fewer. But even though physical strength may be reducing, many in this decade have energy to find and do new and interesting things and they integrate and are psychologically healthy
The 'middle-aged' old	70–79	Now people may feel increasingly isolated as they lose friends or family and robust health. Health problems may intensify and it may be a struggle to maintain their integrated personality as they reduce their involvement in formal structures such as organisations. They may become irritable and may feel stifled and restless
The 'old' old	80–89	People now are likely to find adapting to changed circumstances increasingly difficult. They are likely to need help of some sort to keep up their social and cultural lives
The 'very old' old	90 upwards	This can be a joyful, peaceful and fulfilling time if previous crises have been resolved. People now should be free from responsibility, and able to adapt to enjoy whatever they can even though health problems may become severe or acute.

so on (Cummings 1975). The retirement is likely, because of financial considerations and poorer physical health, to restrict travel and entertainment, and this then contributes to the withdrawal. All this means that the older adult may well become more solitary and likely to retreat into their own inner world – their memories and thoughts. Cummings suggests they will therefore become far less emotional, be psychologically quieter, and spend time reflecting on themselves and their own lives.

The disengagement is seen to have three stages or components:

1. First, shrinkage of life space – which is the reduction in social interaction and social group as people age, and the reduction also in the ageing adult's social roles.
2. Secondly, increased individuality – which is the reduction in social rules, norms and expectations which the older adult has to follow, leading to either a sense of freedom or a sense of confusion. Jenny Joseph's well-known poem about looking forward to old age and a purple hat is a lovely and positive example of this idea.
3. Thirdly, acceptance or embrace of the above changes – leading to a voluntary withdrawal and an acceptance that this is both natural and unavoidable and an appropriate way to behave. This could be illustrated by the well-known, though not always well-practised, phrase of *growing old gracefully*.

How true these ideas are is debatable, especially among modern older adults many of whom seem to be having a very good life still, and who seem to be doing the reverse of withdrawing from society. For example, a new part of the travel and tourism industry is focusing on the so-called 'grey' cohort who have reasonable or good pensions and health and who wish to engage, not disengage, with life for as long as possible. The SAGA holiday brochures, aimed at the over-50s, are full of exciting holidays worldwide. And we also have the term 'silver surfers' used to describe those older adults who use the internet – an interest not usually associated with disengaging from life or interests. So Cumming and Henry's research may have been another example of what we call a 'child of its time', something which has relevance in its own time context rather than a general and generalisable truth.

Research evidence

The theory was based on evidence from a five-year study in Kansas City, USA. The sample was 275 people aged 50–90, and Cummings and Henry observed that as people age they reduce the number of their relationships, and alter the quality of those they keep. This could be a natural and sensible withdrawal from life, a move towards the inevitable death which awaits and which is the final disengagement. It has even been seen as a way for society and the community to renew itself, as the older adults disengage and then die and so make way for younger people (Bromley 1998). Of course, such explanations can also be seen as justifying the isolation and negative attitudes which older adults all too often suffer in our culture, a step towards a Brave New World (Huxley 1932), and Bromley (1998) suggests that the theory could even encourage ageist beliefs and behaviours such as old age having no value.

Havighurst *et al.* (1968) managed to follow up about half of Cumming and Henry's sample and found that those elderly people who did not disengage but stayed engaged in life and maintained activity showed high levels of contentment, with the happiest being the most active.

Progress exercise

See if you can list 2 or 3 pros and 2 or 3 cons for each of the above theories. Then look at what you have written; which theory do you think best explains older adult development, and what makes you think this?

Life events in older adults

Events associated with old age include retirement, bereavement and approaching death. These are discussed later in this chapter. It is very true that retirement can happen to younger people, and there are some extreme cases where people who have become suddenly very wealthy, whether from their own efforts or from something like the National Lottery, take the opportunity to retire. However, these people are far from the norm! And sadly bereavement can strike anyone, at any age. But these events are linked to old age because they are much more likely to happen, or to happen more frequently, at this time of life.

Unemployment, though a feature of most older adults, is foreseen and planned for as retirement, discussed later on in this chapter. Unemployment in younger adults is not at all the same, not usually being either anticipated or planned for. This can be a very difficult, even tragic, life event for younger adults as the lack of paid work eats away at vital self-esteem and self-worth, and at the way others perceive us. It is unwelcome and all too often degrading, whereas retirement can be both welcome and life-enhancing.

Retirement

This can be one of the greatest challenges a person faces as they grow older. This could be because of social stereotypes and norms in our society, as many people have their self-worth and ideas of others' self-worth closely tied to their function or role in employment, rather than to personal features. Many jobs have had an upper age limit beyond which one can no longer be employed, but this was set when people had less chance than currently of a healthy and active old age. Soon there will be more over-50s in our communities than under-50s, and in our own British culture it is probable that older adults will need to continue to do paid work whether they wish to do so or not, or the working population will get too small to support the retired population. There is also a trend emerging in western society, though as a minority influence at the moment, to wish to value and use the rich experience of older adults.

Traditional retirement can be said to be a life event in seven stages or phases as in the following Table 4.2 (Atchley 1977).

It is worth noting that no time-scale is given for these suggested phases. Time would be an individual thing, varying from one person to another. Also, in past times the penultimate phases might well have been quite short, but today they are likely to last for one, two or more decades – a significant proportion of a person's life. Already it is anticipated that many of us will live for twenty-five years post-retirement.

The reorientation phase can of course be regarded as a psychological transition between the world of work and retirement. This

Table 4.2 Atchley's retirement phases

Pre-retirement phase	Work is still being enjoyed and no thought is given to retirement
Work disengagement phase	Retirement is approaching fast and some work tasks are handed on to younger colleagues
Honeymoon phase	The new retirement and freedom from the constraints of work are actively enjoyed
Disenchantment phase	Constant free time and fewer responsibilities start to pall, depression may set in
Reorientation phase	Psychological adjustments are made and some activities are taken up again
The adjusted phase	A new way of life is settled into, possibly with some employment or charity work or group activity
The final phase	Illness may arise, the end of life comes closer and approaching death itself is acknowledged

would make the disenchantment phase the crisis which needs to be resolved. This would mean that the key successful transition of retirement would occur where an older adult can maintain their role and therefore their self-worth in some way. This could involve an increased commitment to the family, perhaps being more involved with grandchildren. Alternatively, some occupations lend themselves more easily to a continuing role, such as writing, whether of fiction or fact, or medical work where there are always part-time or charity posts. Many older people do in fact give time to charity and voluntary work which would support self-worth and -esteem as they would still be contributing valuably to their community, and able to have social interactions. In France there is also the université du troisième age, which encourages new directions and interests, as does the university of the third age and the life-long learning schemes in Britain. Such activities would help an older person reorientate and adjust in a positive way.

The idea of an adjusted phase is supported by evidence that for most people who retire their morale remains high (Streib and Schneider 1971) and their general health improves (Bosse *et al.* 1991), and only those forced to retire from ill-health or redundancy or whose circumstances worsen find it an unhappy, stressful time.

Another aspect of retirement is early retirement. Many younger adults are planning to retire from their first career long before they are 60 years old, in order to focus on a different occupation. This may be another paid job, such as a hospital nurse retraining as an alternative therapist, or someone from the armed forces moving into private security or surveillance work. Or it may provide time for an interest to take over, whether this is gardening or family history research, both of which are growth areas.

Cultural differences

Most of the above information on ageing is based on our individualist culture. It needs to be remembered that in many collectivist cultures retirement is a time of rewards, of respect and leisure for an adult life well lived. In a variety of collectivist cultures from traditional Africa to China the elderly are held in respect, cared for, consulted and looked up to. Traditionally in Chinese culture older family members were cherished and given a comfortable time. Grandparents would be supported by adult children so they could enjoy life. Age in this culture meant veneration. This is typical of collectivism, but not necessarily of the individualism of our own culture where the value of a person may decline when they can no longer contribute visibly so much to their group because of advancing age.

Gender differences

Retirement can also be very different for women. If a woman has spent time at home, has built the life she wants there, then it is a big transition to have her male partner there twenty-four hours a day. It is *his* retirement which is the critical issue. A common account from such women is that they regard home as 'their' territory during the day, and come and go as they please, for example eating lunch or having a small snack or just a cup of tea as they want. But when husbands retire this brings a conflict of expectations if wives wish to continue with their organised and fulfilling lives but husbands think that they should be looked after. This really can be a life crisis for some couples, and can be difficult to resolve. On the other hand, a woman working outside the home could have much the same identity crisis as some men, once their main role, their work role, has ended. Many will want to take up new roles, one sign of a healthy late adulthood, and such people are often the mainstay of charities and other voluntary organisations. Unsurprisingly, retired married women are happiest if their marriages are running smoothly in their retirement (Kim and Moen 1999). However, the same study suggests that male satisfaction in retirement is greater than female. Kim and Moen sampled 534 married men and women in three conditions – about-to-be retired, newly retired and long-term retired. They found that men relished the freedom from work pressure whereas women regretted the loss of their work role. This led to many women being stressed by the transition from work to retirement, and becoming depressed. Some such women may end up far busier as they also care for very aged parents or parents-in-law, becoming caught in the so-called caring trap (Rainey 1998) and this could well contribute significantly to feelings of frustration and lack of satisfaction.

Current thinking is perhaps best reflected by a comment from the occupational psychologist Gary Fitzgibbon (O'Brien 2001) where he says that a successful retirement should be defined by 'what you do next' rather than what was done before, and that a career high point should not be thought of as a ceiling to further happy achievement afterwards or in retirement. He sees it as important that people perceive that life with excitement and fulfilling challenges can and should continue past retirement.

Bereavement

This, always a most sensitive area, may be the most difficult life event for older adults as any bereavement could be seen as a step towards a future where their social circle shrinks and they become more isolated and lonely. A main difficulty can be that while earlier in life bereavements occur only rarely, as we age they are bound to happen increasingly frequently. In the very old there may have been so many bereavements that the old person has few peers left, and can feel very alone because of this. Whatever one's personal beliefs, losing a friend or family member to death is hard, and we experience an emotional state we call grief. Grief has both psychological and physical reactions, and these produce behavioural changes known as mourning. The grieving process may take a considerable length of time, and has recognisable stages.

Bowlby's (1980) stage theory, supported by Parkes (1986), suggests that grieving is related to separation anxiety experienced in childhood. As adults, we may re-experience the anxiety and negativity again as different attachment bonds are broken by death.

A different view is Stroebe *et al.*'s (1993) theory which is based on the social aspects of bereavement. This is not so much a stage theory as a factor theory, and explains bereavement as a four-part loss or a series of losses as follows:

1. Loss of the key or vital social and emotional support from the partner or close friend
2. Loss of the important social validation of one's opinions and judgements once given by the dead person, leading to a loss of personal confidence
3. Loss of support in tasks, loss of material support really, as the bereaved person now has to do all the tasks and activities formerly shared – or give them up
4. Loss of social protection as the partner or friend is no longer there to act as a buffer or comfort the one left when others are unfair or unkind.

Stroebe *et al.* (1993) also argue that total recovery from bereavement may not be possible if the attachment was very deep and meaningful, and say that the grieving can continue for a lifetime. Of course, this failure to recover may also occur if the one left alive is not particularly out-going, or not socially confident. An example of such a person is the twentieth-century British war hero Field Marshal Montgomery, 'Monty' as he was affectionately known, who married late and whose very happy marriage lasted only a few years before his wife died, leaving him withdrawn socially for the rest of his life. This demonstrates that for some individuals the breaking of the emotional bond, the attachment, is indeed a cause of deep psychological trauma.

Table 4.3 Bowlby's four stages of grieving	
Stage	Description
The numbing phase	The person feels numbness and/or disbelief, lasting from hours up to a week, possibly interrupted by intense outbursts of anger and/or distress
Yearning and searching	These feelings of longing for the lost person can last for months or years and can include periods of deep anxiety and anguish
Disorganisation and despair	Depression sets in and the person can become apathetic, even if they are trying to move on emotionally
Reorganisation	Recovery, at least partially, from the bereavement starts as the person begins to accept what has happened

Evaluation

Main critics of these stage and factor theories are Ramsay and de Groot (1977) who put forward the view that grief is more complex, and that the components of grief occur in no fixed order. They suggest there are nine such components or factors, comprising

- shock and numbness
- disorganisation, being unable to make sensible or rational plans
- denial that the person is actually dead
- depression and low moods
- real guilt such as not having done what could quite easily have been done, and unreal guilt such as not having been the perfect partner/friend
- anxiety about how to cope with the future
- aggressive feelings towards people in the situation, such as family members or doctors

- acceptance of the death
- reorganisation of one's life and reintegration into the social world.

Bereavement is also a particularly difficult life event if the death is sudden and unexpected, or the dead person was still young. However, evidence for meaningful bereavement being a traumatic event comes from the subsequent increased health risks, either from stress or from behaviours associated with emotional loss and strain. This ties in closely with Homes and Rahe's SRRS of life events, and is supported by research into stress and health. Examples of bereavement-stress risks include increased accidents, coronary heart disease (CHD), cirrhosis of the liver and violence (Stroebe *et al*. 1993), and also a risk of dying prematurely, especially in those left with a small social network (Gallagher-Thompson *et al*. 1993).

Bereavement and gender

Bereavement is more common in women than in men, for the simple reason that the average male lifespan is shorter than the average female lifespan. Only about 15 per cent of bereaved married people are widowers, the other 85 per cent are widows. In spite of being in the minority and often sought-after, widowers are frequently more depressed than widows and find it more difficult to adjust. This may be because many men have a smaller social circle and socially were very dependent on their wives. It is therefore not so surprising that widowers suffer from more health problems and survive less well than widows (Bury and Holme 1991), even though bereaved men are more likely to remarry than bereaved women. But this latter could be just an effect of the proportions of bereaved men and women, a number thing and not a psychological one.

The darkest view of bereavement is that it is a foretaste, a fore-seeing, of one's own death, and that is why we are brought low when we lose someone. In our own, western culture, the current Zeitgeist seems to be that death is a great taboo subject, and this attitude makes bereavement and grieving more difficult. People are embarrassed to talk or listen about death, and discussion of a person's own future death is considered rather morbid, except in specific contexts. Hospices are one such context, where acceptance of death coming sooner rather than later is turned into a positive experience for the person concerned and hopefully for their family and friends also. This seems to tie in with Erikson's integrity overcoming despair idea, and with other models of people taking stock of their lives and realising that it has, after all, been worthwhile.

This taboo is not universal, though grief itself is. The Victorians accepted death as part of life, a very pragmatic approach from a very practical culture. Their bereavement rituals involved as much show as was affordable, with special black clothes, ornate funerary vehicles and accoutrements, and a whole social time-scale for the outward signs of bereavement. In the present, some tribes in New Guinea still preserve their dead relatives by drying the bodies over smoky fires and then siting these on hillsides overlooking the village, so keeping the person with them at least physically, and lessening the sense of immediate loss which could make coming to terms with its reality less painful. Traditional Chinese culture also has a strong ritual for bereavement, as do very many cultures. From the psychological point of view the use of ritual is thought to be helpful, though not just to older adults, in coping with both bereavement and grieving. It gives a structure and form to behaviour in these circumstances, and an outward sign to others as well so they know what has happened and can respond appropriately.

Cognitive changes in late adulthood (memory and intelligence)

The stereotype of an 'old' person usually includes being forgetful, a bit deaf, mentally slow; all these are cognitive failures and many people accept as fact that they are part of being old. But many teenagers seem to think their parents, though hardly in the eighth Erikson stage, don't remember what they are told, don't hear too well and are a bit slow on the uptake – and that opinion works vice versa too! This makes it more difficult to sort out what we actually truly know about cognitive changes in old people, what good research rather than a stereotypic view supports. Memory and intelligence in the elderly have been researched and this is discussed in this chapter.

Memory and intelligence

A widespread belief is that as a person ages, especially when they are an older adult, their cognitive abilities reduce or decay. Both memory and intelligence are accepted as at risk from ageing, but research evidence does not tie in completely with this belief.

Early research by Wechsler (1958) showed intelligence reaching a peak at about the age of 30. This used Wechsler's own Adult Intelligence Scale or WAIS. But like other similar research Wechsler used cross-sectional studies to compare cognitive abilities across the age-groups. This meant he took representative samples of adults from young adults to the very old. But this method is full of flaws because of the very many extraneous and probably confounding variables between the various groups. Any age-group has its own time context and life experiences, and this will affect how people perform in psychometric tests. People who were young in times of economic stress may have experienced poorer health and diets than other better-off groups, for instance, and this could well have an effect on the brain's development and hence on cognitive ability. Other groups may have had enriched experiences, and this too can affect cognitive ability. So such groups are not comparable. Also, unless a big commitment is made for research funding of longitudinal studies lasting many decades, we don't know how actual individual people change or do not change as they go through life. A few longitudinal studies have been done (Holahan and Sears 1995) which give a different and probably truer picture. They suggest that some people retain their cognitive abilities past middle adulthood, but also that different kinds of intelligence and different kinds of memory do change with age, but in different ways. Burns (1966) discussed a longitudinal study of adults who were tested when aged 22 years and again thirty-four years later. They showed cognitive enhancement as they got older. This supports the reservations about cross-sectional studies, and also raises the idea that as people age they may get better at using their abilities, such as memory or intelligence, rather like the old saying 'practice makes perfect'!

This ties in with a concept which has recently attracted renewed attention, the concept of two types of intelligence, fluid and crystallised (Cattell 1963). These can be tested for quite easily (Kline 1992). Fluid intelligence is made up of basic reasoning skills, that are 'nature', i.e.

genetic in origin and not much affected by a person's environment, whereas crystallised intelligence is a 'nurture' ability and definitely is affected by environment as well as being culture-dependent. Basically, what is suggested is that in older adults their brain-processing abilities may be slowed down and they may therefore appear less intelligent than formerly, less intelligent than younger adults, but that the years of experience enable many older adults to compensate for this by using skills and strategies they have learned. This concept certainly has some face validity. It seems likely, common-sensical, that fluid intelligence reduces or slows down with age especially if it is measured or tested using problem-solving of novel or unusual or abstract situations. On the other hand, crystallised intelligence should increase as people age, right up to the end of life unless senility intervenes (Horn 1982). People amass knowledge all through life and so can develop and refine cognitive abilities, make new schemata – mental representations of their world and society, and so on. There is also evidence that keeping on using cognitive skills maintains and develops them, so that seemingly simple things like regularly doing word and other puzzles, playing card games, taking part in social events and other activities will be supporting crystallised intelligence even if processing speeds are slowing. There is much support for this idea, including Rogers *et al.* (1990), and Denney and Palmer (1981), as well as for the slowing of fluid intelligence (Schaie and Hetzog 1983), while Cavanaugh (1995) also points out that people may well not be expected to use their fluid intelligence so much as they age. We, their community, may not be doing people a good turn by expecting less of them!

Progress exercise

What evidence could you yourself suggest to support the ideas given above about older adults and their cognitive abilities, their fluid and crystallised intelligences?

Senility and Alzheimer's disease

Senility is the term for the partial collapse of abilities in old age. It is generally thought to be the breakdown of normal brain processing due to age, as neurons malfunction or cease to function, much as a machine's parts wear out with time. Alzheimer's disease is different. It is the most common form of dementia and does, like senility, involve memory loss. It is a specific disease involving a breakdown of the hippocampus, a tiny part of the cortex with a deep involvement in memory and processing information such as emotions, as well as a more general loss of neurons which are replaced by fibrous tissue. Typically, Alzheimer patients develop progressive memory loss and also seem emotionally confused, as described so movingly in John Bayley's book about the last years of his wife, the novelist Iris Murdoch. The hippocampus and its surrounding area in the medial temporal lobe of the cortex slowly shrink with age, but in Alzheimer's the shrinkage is ten times more rapid. This is a frightening disorder, and one which is increasing as our population ages. But still, for most people, psychology suggests that the mental decline in late adulthood needs to be rejected as an inevitable part of growing old, and this negative stereotype needs firm refuting. The cultural nature of this stereotype and its negative and ageist effects are shown in studies such as Levy and Langer (1994). They compared communities in mainland China with both deaf and hearing people in the USA. Their assumption was that older people are more valued in Chinese society than in American culture, but that deaf Americans would be less exposed than their hearing compatriots to ageist beliefs. The results supported this idea. Not only were memory tasks done better by older Chinese and deaf Americans than by hearing Americans, but also they found a positive correlation between beliefs and attitudes about ageing and performance on memory tasks. Now this of course cannot infer any causation between beliefs and memory ability, but it hints that there is a possibility of the belief being a self-fulfilling prophesy in either direction. Hopefully this might encourage people in western culture to have higher expectations and positive stereotypes of growing old, and of older adults.

Cultural variations in ageing

As said before in this chapter, most collectivist cultures value older adults far more than individualist cultures do. However, there are exceptions. In our own, western, individualist culture it is always remarked on if a person achieves leader status and they are still relatively young. This hints at a conflict in our perceptions, assumptions and stereotypes. On the one hand, we seem to value youth, and what it stands for, and comment negatively on signs of age, such as baldness in political leaders. Yet on the other hand we express surprise if a leader is young, as though youth here is strange. If youth is desired and attractive, then to associate leadership with age is odd. Yet age does also carry an aura of experience and wisdom. This is an anomaly, and probably typical of human life and human beliefs! It is also an example of cognitive dissonance.

Worldwide, age is not negatively perceived. A review in 1989 (Tout) shows that older adults keep their authority and status and social inclusion in many societies, but in western, industrialised cultures growing older does promote social differentiation (Keith 1977). Even within Europe there are large differences in the attitudes and behaviours towards older people. Greek culture holds the belief that people remain vigorous into their late 70s and maybe longer, so they stay in the community (Amira 1990). But in Denmark (Jamieson 1990) the state takes older people out of their community to care for them, but in doing so isolates them. And looking further afield, not all collectivist cultures value old age. Tout (1989) found that in nomadic peoples the elderly are not regarded with respect as their mobility difficulties are a serious problem for their tribe, hindering moving on and therefore survival. Turnbull (1989) reports that the Ik! people of Uganda show much negativity towards their elderly, though that may well be a result of their own problems from the difficult and hostile social and economic environment they have suffered.

In the far east, in India and China for instance, the traditional stereotypes and behaviours valuing older adults is still apparent, though it may be changing as a result of increased exposure to western culture as portrayed by the media.

Ageing happily

Finally, a word about happy ageing. Psychological research often ignores looking at factors which increase happiness, and indeed the research in older adults and ageing throws up many less pleasant aspects of growing older. But many older people are happy, and this is likely to be related to their physical health, financial security and also, as Havighurst (1964) suggests, their level of social activity. This research looked across cultures and found that social isolation was a real predictor of unhappy ageing. This means that good involvement with family, friends and community increases a person's chance of feeling positive, whatever their actual age, as Michael Argyle (2001) has said. Being older does not mean people cease to want to feel they matter! If older adults continue to feel good self-worth they are more likely to be happy, and also to bother to take care of themselves, which in turn will maintain their health and well-being.

What new or adapted roles can you think of which an older adult could take on and develop, in order to keep happy and psychologically healthy, even if they are physically not as strong as they were?

Progress exercise

Further reading

http://www.apa.org/pi/aging/summary.html is a collection of varied summaries about psychological issues and older adults, a record of presentations to the American Congress in 2002.

http://www.apa.org/releases/aging_memory.html is an account of intriguing research showing that older adults have fewer negative memories than younger adults.

5

Alternative theories

⬕ Humanistic theory and adult development
◈ Psychodynamic view on ageing
⬔ Alternative approaches explaining ageing

Humanistic theory and adult development

This movement developed in the USA in the 1960s and was a gestalt type of approach, looking at the wholeness of each human being. It also based itself on the belief that we all have free will and that this is conscious, i.e. we choose freely and consciously when we make decisions, however small these may be. This approach was a reaction against and a rejection of the dehumanising and/or deterministic ideas of behaviourism and psychodynamic theory, and represented a positive and hopeful view of ourselves including ageing. The first humanistic psychologists included Bugental, Rogers and Maslow, and they aimed for an approach which could truly understand and describe a complete human being, what today might be called an holistic approach.

Key assumptions of humanistic theory:

- only individual people should be studied as we are each of us unique, i.e. explanations about ourselves should be **idiographic**, not **nomothetic**
- there is no point studying non-human animals as they are not people

- research should address areas of human life which are meaningful
- research should be applied to enrich real lives
- research needs to include **introspection**, internal experience, and allow for people to exercise **free will**
- the whole person should be studied, in personal, real-life contexts.

When this approach is applied to ageing it suggests that our self-concept, our sense of identity, is crucial to our well-being in old age. Roger's self theory makes this quite clear, though he did not write specifically about personality and self-identity in older adults. But at any age if the theory is correct it must be true that how we see ourselves, psychologically, will affect our beliefs and behaviours profoundly, so if people associate ageing with negative factors then they will have an increasingly negative self-image as they age – but if they associate growing old with positive factors then they are much more likely to age happily and positively. You can already see that this is a very different way from the classic stage or crisis approaches of looking at ageing.

Maslow's **hierarchy of needs**, and the ideas of self-actualisation are also important in ageing. If we do journey through life seeking to supply our needs and develop our potential then there is no cut-off point such as reaching a certain age; the journey would be life-long. This would suggest that we continue to have needs as long as we live, not just for staying alive – food, shelter, health – but also aesthetic and intellectual and social needs. This sounds very like common sense – an approach with face validity. A key point of Maslow's model is that the various needs we have will vary, and it seems clear that one variation will be related to age. A child's needs, whether basic, aesthetic or whatever, will differ from those of a young adult, and differ again from the needs of an older person. People do say, as they grow older, that their choices change, including their choice of friends and of pursuits. This fits in well with Maslow's hierarchy model.

Humanistic theory also has its own spin on the concept of abnormality. It suggests that what society labels as abnormal may be an imposing of low value, what they call low conditions of worth. This also could fit in with what is experienced by older adults in our communities. It suggests that what we do not value, what we hold in low esteem or low worth, we can call abnormal and then use this label as a justification of ignoring these aspects of life. So in a community

Maslow's hierarchy of needs

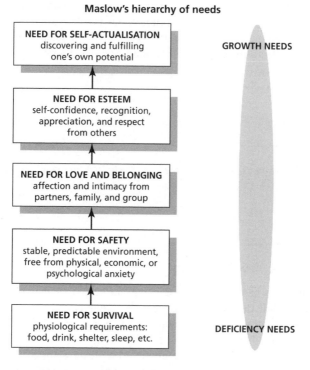

Figure 5.1 Maslow's hierarchy of needs

where older adults are not valued and have low worth, their needs will be more likely to be ignored and their beings and behaviours will be regarded askance, or disregarded, and labelled as abnormal. Older adults' slower mental processing or memory, for instance, may be labelled as abnormal, and then disregarded as there isn't anything to be done for the problem because it is abnormal. So these older people are the victims of a circular argument based on a faulty assumption. This illustrates the nomothetic approach which humanistic theory is so against. To humanistic psychologists ageing is, like anything else, a personal thing, and so what is truly abnormal in one person is not relevant to another person. This other person will have their own, unique life and personality and lifespan development.

What the humanistic approach brings to the psychological study of adulthood and ageing is humanity. It looks at us as individuals and puts importance on individual consciousness, and emphasises personal development or actualisation and choice. But it is also culturally biased in that it is too clearly based on the western individualist culture, and ignores collectivist cultures. Furthermore, it is also founded on beliefs such as free will and consciousness which are extremely difficult to study objectively or empirically.

Progress exercise

Which two humanistic assumptions do you feel are the most important ones, and what are your reasons for thinking so?

Psychodynamic view on ageing

This theory is based on Freud's thinking and teaching. It does not really address adult development, except in a roundabout way. This is because it suggests that our adult life is beset with problems and/ or problem behaviours which have their origins in the frustrations, anxieties and conflicts of our infant years. It does suggest that by using psychoanalysis these underlying causes of unhappiness or dissatisfaction in adulthood can be identified, confronted and overcome. This is not really an approach which contributes a lot to lifespan psychology, the study of how we develop as we age, because classic psychodynamic theory assumes that most of our psychological development is completed by the time we are young adults, and that further development is minor. It is also a speculative approach, being based on hypothetical constructs such as Freud's psychosexual development stages, most of which are very difficult indeed, if at all possible, to research objectively or empirically. Perhaps the main contribution to lifespan psychology from the psychodynamic approach is that it has led to the modern assumption that we have unconscious motives and desires, that at any age we can do or not do, want or not want, speak or be silent – for an apparent reason which we may later realise was not the real reason. In other words we may hide our true feelings or aims from ourselves, at any age.

Try and write three or four sentences explaining support for Freud's ideas on ageing.

Alternative approaches explaining ageing

Personality and ageing

This concept suggests that older adults' life experiences could depend on individual personality types or traits but it does not identify whether these types are innate, i.e. **nature**, or the result of learning, i.e. **nurture**.

Reichard *et al.* (1962) researched a relatively small group of Americans aged 55–84 years. They interviewed them and analysed the reports and found five personality types with associated attitudes and coping strategies for growing older.

This personality type theory does give useful descriptions of how different beliefs and attitudes can affect behaviour in older adults, but this is not informative as to how those beliefs and attitudes evolved. It is also acknowledged that smaller samples are not likely to be representative of the general population, thus limiting how the findings can be applied usefully. This means that though this personality theory has some interest it is not really a lifespan approach even within western culture as it focuses on only one adult period.

Family life cycle

This is based on Duval's (1971) model. This suggests an eight-stage pattern to adult life, and allows for individual differences by saying that each 'family' will progress through the stages at its own speed, spending shorter or longer periods of time per stage as appropriate. Each stage makes its own demands on the members of the family. Evidence comes from interviews, such as by Galinsky (1981).

Table 5.1 Reichard et al.'s five personality types	
Personality type	**Adjustment to growing older**
Hostile: external locus of control with others being blamed for one's own problems	Poor
Hostile: internal locus of control with oneself being blamed for one's own difficulties	Poor
Constructive: has come to terms with the problems of growing older and is interacting positively with others	Good
Dependent: regards old age as a time for leisure and relying on others for any help which may be needed	Good
Defensive: continuing to act much as before with no allowance made for growing older	Good (for the time being)

This model has been useful in describing standard, western family life, though the western bias means it is not generalisable to other cultures or sub-cultures, or many partnering or family arrangements today. One example of this is the ignoring of sequential families as a result of bereavement or divorce, or of single-parent families, both of which types are becoming increasingly common. It describes suggested stages in family life without details of how and why adults develop and change in different ways. It would also not apply to the increasing number of adults who do not have children, whatever their reason, whether or not they are in a couple relationship. This means that though this concept does fit the lifespan mode it focuses on a narrow target population and is descriptive rather than explanatory.

Table 5.2 Family stage theory		
Stage	Family content	Comments
1. Honeymoon	Married/cohabiting couples with no children	This is usually seen, retrospectively, as the happiest time, maybe because responsibilities were lowest, and the couple could spend time and energy on their own relationship
2. Nurturing	Families with child(ren), the eldest child being under 2 years old	The demands on the adults are considerable and usually unexpectedly high. The level of tiredness was often not anticipated, even though the adults are delighted with the child(ren)
3. Authority	Pre-school families, the eldest child(ren) being 2–5 years old	The adults are working out how to manage the child(ren) and also their own contributions to family responsibilities and shared authority
4. Interpretive	School-age families with the eldest child(ren) being 5–13 years old	Adults say they become more realistic about the family now. They focus on interpreting, broadening and balancing child experiences
5. Interdependent	Families with teenagers at home	Significant changes within the family may occur with the adult relationship strengthening as a result to cope

continued

Table 5.2 continued		
Stage	Family content	Comments
6. Launching	Young adults leaving the family, first child leaving to last child leaving	Very variable. Sometimes this stage is stressful, other times easy. Most stress is reported if children do not leave as expected (Datan *et al.* 1987)
7. Empty-nest	Middle-aged parents, no children living at home	Some couples experience stress, where the children, now gone from the family home, held the couple's relationship together. Others find great happiness reaffirming their own relationship, sharing new interests and enjoyment. This can be the happiest time (Argyle 1990)
8. Retirement	Ageing adults, retired from paid employment	This may in fact be the longest stage as regards duration

Further reading

http://www.apa.org/monitor/jun05/juggle.html (2005) describes Canadian research which suggests that older adults need to focus more of their attention on multiple tasks than younger adults do, because they find such tasks increasingly difficult.

http://www.apa.org/releases/education_aging.html (2005) shows how having had higher education benefits the older adult, supported by evidence from brain imaging studies.

6

Student essays with examiner's comments

Essay 1

> **Discuss research relating to gender *and/or* cultural differences in two aspects of adult relationships (e.g. marriage, divorce, parenthood). (24 marks)**

Starting point

As in all questions you are required to present an equal amount of description (AO1) and commentary (AO2) – the injunction 'discuss' tells you to describe and evaluate. The next key word is 'research', meaning that your study should be focused on appropriate studies or theories. This research must be related to gender differences.

The final part of the question indicates that you must cover two aspects of relationships. Three examples are given (taken from the specification) but if you do cover all three you will only get credit for the best two. If you only cover one then your answer will be marked out of a total of 18 marks rather than 24 (partial performance).

Always remember that, in order to attract top marks, it is important to demonstrate a balance between depth and breadth – if you try to discuss too many studies/theories ('breadth') you won't have time for sufficient detail and elaboration (the 'depth'). Always be selective and do justice to those studies/theories you do cover.

Student's answer

The concept of gender differences implies that in certain behaviours there are real differences in the way males and females behave. How true is this assumption? Well, it can be illustrated using research into marriage and divorce.

Some theories of types of marriage have differentiated between those marriages in which the male is the dominant partner, and others where there is more of a partnership between male and female partners. For example, Duberman (1973) identified the traditional marriage as the former, and companionship and colleague marriages as the latter. But this does not tell us whether both genders were equally satisfied with their type of marriage.

Research of the 1970s such as Bernard's, and Veroff and Feld's, showed that married men are more satisfied, happier than either married women or single men. So how does this fit in with Argyle's view, confirmed by Bee and the Rutters, that marriage brings increased social and emotional support which would surely increase happiness? It could be that this support is not perceived to be provided equally by males and females. In other words, if the support by males was not satisfactory, but that from females was, this could explain the different levels of happiness.

But can psychology suggest why there is this difference in support? It could be that women have been brought up to be the nurturers, meaning that this is learned behaviour; alternatively this could actually be innate behaviour, nature not nurture. It is true that in western society females do what is sometimes called 'tend and befriend' behaviours, especially when a person is stressed or upset in some way. Men do not seem to practise this behaviour, but this still does not tell us if this behaviour and difference are innate or learned. Research from as early as the 1960s has shown that in our culture women probably have to make more adjustments to their lives when they marry than men do. This is because their role changes and they become less dominant.

Unfortunately, there are some methodological reservations about the data in this sort of research. Mostly it has been gathered by questionnaires and surveys, and we know that this means the data are not particularly reliable and perhaps may not have strong internal validity. This is because we cannot verify the data. We have no way of knowing how truthful or open participants are, nor whether their responses have been 'edited' by social desirability, nor how accurate their memories are either, especially as we know that memories can naturally reconstruct over time.

Do these gender differences also apply to divorce? It seems they do, because men's greater satisfaction with marriage is supported by their greater frequency of remarriage following divorce. We assume that they are seeking a return to their happier, married state. Research also supports the idea that divorce is more stressful for women, which might deter them from entering into a subsequent marriage. However, the effects of divorce are worse for men. This is interesting, because at first this does not seem to fit the previous research. But as we know from studies on managing stress, women cope better probably because they have more meaningful or just larger social support networks than men. So though they find stress more upsetting, women might survive this better because of their support networks.

Examiner's comments

This is a clearly written response, a bit on the short side for a 30-minute answer but well focused on the question. The candidate has covered two aspects of adult relationships: marriage and divorce though there is some imbalance. It is possible to gain full marks even when the two things are not balanced but you do need to provide sufficient detail of both aspects – which is not the case here.

The first paragraph is a brief introduction, which doesn't receive any credit as such but contributes to the overall structure. Paragraph 2 is mainly AO1 with a brief comment at the end, lacking elaboration. Paragraph 3 contains a good mix of AO1 and AO2. In paragraph 4 the theory has been used as AO2 and the final paragraph on marriage is all AO2 (methodological criticism).

The paragraph on divorce is again a good mix of AO1 and AO2 (commentary starts from 'This is interesting . . .').

Overall the AO1 content lies between band 2 and 3: limited/slightly limited content, reasonably detailed, coherent, evidence of depth and breadth but imbalanced. The AO2 is of an equivalent standard, perhaps slightly less impressive.

This essay would receive 9 (description) + 8 (evaluation) = 17/24, which is equivalent to a Grade A.

Essay 2

> (a) Outline research into how people cope with bereavement (12 marks)
>
> (b) To what extent are there cultural differences in how people cope with bereavement? (12 marks)

Starting point

This is a parted question where all the AO1 marks are in part (a) and all the AO2 marks are in part (b) ('to what extent' is an AO2 injunction). So in part (a) you should describe research (theories and/or studies) on bereavement. The injunction used is 'outline' which indicates that you may not have to give the same amount of depth as when 'describe' is used as the AO1 injunction but you still must give some details and not just a 'shopping list' of relevant research. It is often tempting, in such parted questions, to mention some of the evaluation points related to the research you are outlining. There would be no credit for such information in part (a). However, if it was relevant to part (b), the examiner may 'export' it for the purpose of determining marks. BUT it is unlikely to be relevant here because the AO2 requirements are quite specific for part (b).

The injunction 'to what extent' is a tricky one because there is a temptation to describe *cultural differences in how people cope with bereavement but this is not what is required. You must use your knowledge of cultural differences in how people cope with bereavement to consider the extent to which there are differences. You do not need to reach any conclusion(s) but just consider whether there are differences, with reference to evidence, and you might also consider whether there are similarities, again with reference to evidence.*

Student's answer

(a) Several psychological models of bereavement suggest this is a grieving process taking place in stages. For example, Bowlby and Parkes each suggested the trauma of bereavement relates to separation anxiety learned in early childhood. The loss by death reawakens this behaviour, and the stages are Numbing, Yearning and Searching, Disorganisation and Despair, and if the bereaved person recovers, then

Reorganisation. This is quite psychodynamic in its approach, as it is suggesting that behaviour in adulthood is determined by early childhood experiences.

On the other hand, Kubler-Ross researched bereavement extensively and thought that this is a natural and necessary behaviour. Her stages are as follows: Denial, followed by Anger, then what she called Bargaining, Depression and then if there is a positive outcome, Acceptance of the loss.

Stroebe has a different approach, focusing on social factors rather than stages. All these factors refer to losses as follows, of Social and emotional support, of Social validation, of Tasks and material support, and of Social protection. She argues that if a relationship was deeply meaningful then the bereaved person may never actually achieve full recovery. In her later work, Kubler-Ross agreed that each individual moves through bereavement at their own pace and in their own way, and may move through all, some or none of her suggested stages and in any order.

(b) Gender culture has an effect on bereavement, as social norms affect how the two genders behave. Male culture in the western world is more macho, and so does not allow for much expression of grieving, and this could be the reason why widowers are more likely to be depressed than widows. Also, in traditional western culture men would not have been so used to looking after themselves and their homes, as this is seen as women's work, and so might just be finding it harder to cope with the mechanics of everyday life than women would. This might well explain another finding, that widowers have worse health and a shorter lifespan than widows, though this could just fit in with the fact that women naturally live longer than men anyway. However, Stroebe's theory does suggest real gender culture differences which would affect bereavement. She thinks that there are two behaviours which are needed for successfully coping with bereavement, and that while women do both these, i.e. they deal with the emotional issues as well as seeking distractions, men focus mainly on the distractions and neglect the emotional issues.

What about religious or social culture? Well, research suggests that both western and eastern religions seem to believe in a higher power, a spiritual power which orders life and gives it meaning and suggests that death here is not the end of everything. This belief and its attendant ritual for dealing with death are very comforting when a person is bereaved, and gives them hope and a structure so they can cope better with their loss. Golden supports this view, as he suggest there is the chaos butterfly effect, which means that from one small (in the sense of in the world) event, i.e. a death, a huge wave of grief and bereavement behaviours can spread out. However, if a person has a ritual this can help them cope with this chaos. In fact, it makes the bereavement a lot less chaotic. The cultural ritual gives permission, in a way, for them to show their pain and trauma, and provides a format which others will recognise. Furthermore, if there is no religious culture, Golden suggests other non-religious rituals can apply, such as looking at a record of the dead person's life, in photos maybe, or holding a celebratory wake. Other research also supports this concept of rituals as different cultures often have a kind of time plan for bereavement, such as the traditional Jewish 12-month plan, or the Victorian social ritual where bereaved women would wear only black clothes for a year, and then move into grey and shades of purple, and then slowly introduce other quiet colours if they felt their grief was subsiding.

What does this all mean? It seems that bereavement grief is universal, and so it is innate in us humans. Furthermore, we have in various different cultures constructed ways, successful or less successful of trying to deal with bereavement. So bereavement and grieving are normal and natural, genetic, but how we deal with them varies from individual to individual but also from culture to culture, both belief-based and social norm-based ones.

Examiner's comments

Bowlby's theory is succinctly outlined as required in the question, whereas the second theory (Kubler-Ross) is only given basic/rudimentary coverage. The final paragraph is somewhat muddled. Altogether part (a) is rather short and would be described as reasonably constructed, some evidence of breadth and depth, lacking detail but at least it is focused on the question: 5 or 6 marks. It reads too much like a shopping list.

Part (b) starts with commentary on gender. In order for gender to be creditworthy in an essay on cultural differences a clear argument needs to be presented as to why gender is an example of culture. Saying 'gender culture' is not sufficient. However, in subsequent sentences the candidate is actually talking about cultural differences in male/female behaviour so the material is potentially appropriate; however, *there is no attempt to discuss other cultures so it is not entirely clear what the differences are. Overall this paragraph is at best reasonably effective in relation to the essay title.*

The second paragraph is much more effective. Differences between cultures are considered, with relevant psychological support and the focus is on the extent of the differences rather than just describing them (though inevitably there is a certain amount of description).

The final paragraph is an attempt to interpret the evidence – a valid way to achieve AO2 marks . . . except the candidate says that bereavement grief is universal and this evidence hasn't been explicitly explored. Thus, the final paragraph is not fully effective as some important evidence seems to have been skipped.

The AO2 content is a mixed bag and ends up only as a reasonably effective 7 or 8 marks. The AO2 is better than the AO1.

This essay would receive 8 (description) + 5 (evaluation) (or 7+6) = 13/24, which is equivalent to a weak Grade C.

Glossary

ageism is the attitude and/or behaviour prejudiced or biased against certain age-groups and in favour of other age-groups

androcentric bias is bias in favour of males, and therefore against females

collectivist cultures believe in the importance and survival of the group above that of the individual, and in cooperation and interdependence, unlike individualist cultures

Dream, the is Levinson's concept of a person's view of themselves in the adult world together with a plan for adult life, stretching into the future

dynamic describes something which changes, evolves, does not stay the same, such as relationships or social norms

ethnocentrism is a biased focus on one culture so that its values, norms and research findings are wrongly generalised to other cultures leading to faulty interpretations and conclusions about the other cultures, because cross-cultural differences are ignored or misunderstood

Eurocentric is the biased ethnocentric focus on European culture, common in much twentieth-century psychological research

face validity or surface validity refers to research or concepts which seem to make sense in the everyday world

false assumptions are just that – assumptions which are accepted but are actually untrue

free will is the concept that we humans are free to choose our behaviours, and are not controlled in any way

gender differences are those differences which occur between males and females

generativity is Erikson's concept of 'establishing and guiding the next generation', through becoming a parent or through creativity or altruism

hierarchy of needs is Maslow's concept of a graded progression of motivations for human behaviours

hunter-gatherer ancestors are our long-gone human ancestors who lived, 50,000 to 100,000 years ago, by hunting and gathering food and materials

idiographic approaches are based on the uniqueness of the individual person, and which therefore do not see any sense in generalising from a sample of people to a group as every person is so different from everyone else

individualist cultures believe in independence, competition and therefore the survival of the fittest, unlike collectivist cultures

innate means inborn, and usually refers to a behaviour which is genetically determined and not learned

introspection was a popular tool early on in psychological research, and involved being aware of and examining one's own thought processes

life cycle is Levinson's idea of the four parts or seasons in a person's lifespan

life events are those significant and major changes in life, such as starting school, falling in love or losing someone dear

life structure is Levinson's concept of a basic pattern or plan, common to all humans, which is followed through life

longitudinal studies investigate the same participants over a long period of time, sometimes many years, though this is difficult and expensive to do

Mid-life crisis describes a suggested psychological crisis which may occur mid-way in the lifespan, i.e. in the 40s of 50s, where the person questions assumptions or plans about their life and their future

nature in the nature–nurture debate describes the influence on human behaviour from our inherited genes, our hormones, neurochemicals and brain function

The **nomothetic** approach accepts that humans are basically similar and therefore can be compared, and samples can be studied and the findings generalised to the population at large

nurture in the nature-nurture debate describes the influence on human behaviour from our learning and experiences, from our environment

reliability is the concept that research is consistent, that we can rely on methods to give consistent findings which we can then trust to be accurate and therefore generalisable more widely, including over time

separation anxieties are those stemming from early childhood separations which lead people to fear future separations, even in adult life

social desirability bias is the natural desire of individuals to appear as socially acceptable as possible; and this may make then alter their behaviours and responses when being studied. This of course makes the research less valid

The **sociobiological** approach bases the study of human behaviour, particularly social behaviour, on evolutionary principles, so it is extremely biological and a 'nature' view

time context describes a behaviour or whatever is being studied in the context of its time. This could be its decade, century, year or social period. It suggests that the social and other norms of that time are an important influence on behaviours

transitions are Levinson's terms for the overlapping periods of time as an individual moves from one life stage, e.g. early adulthood, to the next life stage, e.g. middle adulthood

validity is the description of whether a method of research is actually measuring in some way what it intended to measure. There are two main types; internal validity refers to whether the findings relate directly to the variables set by the researchers, and external validity refers to whether the findings would be consistent if other environments or participants were used

References

Alibhai-Brown, Y. (2000) *Who Do We Think We Are? Imagining the New Britain*. London: Penguin.

American Psychological Association (APA) (2006) *Sexual Orientation, Parents and Children*. http://www.apa.org/pi/lgbc/policy/parents.html online 1 May 2006.

Amira, A. (1990) Family care in Greece. In A. Jamieson and R. Illsley, (eds), *Contrasting European Policies for the Care of Older People*. Aldershot: Avebury Press.

Argyle, M. (1983) *The Social Psychology of Interpersonal Behaviour*. Harmondsworth: Penguin.

Argyle, M. (1990) Relationships. Lecture delivered at the Psychology Teachers' Updating Workshop, Oxford.

Argyle, M. (2001) *The Psychology of Happiness*. London: Taylor and Francis.

Argyle, M. and Furnham, A. (1983) Sources of satisfaction and conflict in long-term relationships. *Journal of Marriage and the Family* 45, 481–93.

Argyle, M. and Henderson, M. (1985) *The Anatomy of Relationships: And the Rules and Skills Needed to Handle Them Successfully*. Harmondsworth: Penguin.

Atchley, R. (1977) *The Sociology of Retirement*. Cambridge, MA: Schenkman.

Bandura, A. (1970) Modeling theory: Some traditions, trends, and disputes. In W. S. Sahakian (ed.), *Psychology of Learning: Systems, Models, and Theories*. Chicago: Markham. (Reprinted in, R. D. Parke (ed.), *Recent Trends in Social Learning Theory*. New York: Academic Press, 1972.)

Bee, H. (1994) *Lifespan Development*. New York: HarperCollins.

Bee, H. (1998) *The Journey of Adulthood*, 3rd edn. Upper Saddle River, NJ: Prentice-Hall.

Benedek, T. (1959) Parenthood as a developmental phase. *Journal of the American Psychoanalytic Association* 7, 389–417.

Bengston, V. L., Rosenthal, C. and Burton, L. (1990) Families and aging: Diversity and heterogeneity. In R. H. Binstock and L. K. George (eds), *Handbook of Aging and the Social Sciences*, 3rd edn. San Diego, CA: Academic Press.

Berk, L. E. (1998) *Development through the Lifespan*. London: Allyn and Bacon.

Bernard, J. (1972) *The Future of Marriage*. New Haven: Yale University Press.

Bigner, J. J. and Jacobsen, R. B. (1989) The value of children to gay and heterosexual fathers. *Journal of Homosexuality* 18(1–2), 163–72.

Bisagni, G. M. and Eckenrode, J. (1995) The role of work identity in women's adjustment to divorce. *American Journal of Orthopsychiatry* 65 (4), 574–83.

Bohannon, P. (1970) *Divorce and After*. New York: Doubleday.

Bosse, R., Aldwin, C. M., Levenson, M. R. and Workman-Daniels, K. (1991) How stressful is retirement? Findings from the Normative Aging Study. *Journal of Gerontology* 46 (1), 9–14.

Bowlby, J. (1980) *Attachment and Loss*, vol. III: *Loss, Sadness and Depression*. London: Hogarth.

Bradburn, N. (1969) *The Structure of Psychological Well-being*. Chicago: Aldine.

Bromley, D. B. (1998) *Human Ageing: An Introduction to Gerontology*, 3rd edn. Harmondsworth: Penguin.

Burns, R. B. (1966) Age and mental ability. *British Journal of Educational Psychology* 36, 116.

Burnside, I. M., Ebersole, P. and Monea, H. E. (1979) *Psychological Caring throughout the Lifespan*. New York: McGraw-Hill.

Bury, M. and Holme, A. (1991) *Life after Ninety*. London: Routledge.

Buunk, B. P. (1996) Affiliation, attraction and close relationships. In

M. Hewstone, W. Stroebe, and G. M. Stephenson (eds), *Introduction to Social Psychology*, 2nd edn. Oxford: Blackwell.

Cattell, R. B. (1963) Theory of fluid and crystallized intelligence: A critical experiment. *Journal of Educational Psychology* 54, 1–22.

Cavanaugh, J. C. (1995) Ageing. In P. E. Bryant and A. M. Colman (eds), *Developmental Psychology*. London: Longman.

Cochrane, R. (1988) Marriage, separation and divorce. In S. Fisher and J. Reason (eds), *Handbook of Life Stress, Cognition and Health*. Chichester: Wiley.

Cohen, S. and Hoberman, H. M. (1983) Positive events and social supports as buffers of life change stress. *Journal of Applied Social Psychology* 13, 99–125.

Coleman, J. C. (1978) Current contradictions in adolescent theory. *Journal of Youth & Adolescence* 7, 1–11.

Coleman, J. C. (1980) Friendship and the peer group in adolescence. In J. Adelson (ed.), *Handbook of Adolescent Psychology*. New York: Wiley.

Cooper, G. (1996) The satisfying side of being home alone. *Independent*, 13 September, 3.

Cox, M. J., Paley, B., Burchinal, M. and Payne, C. (1999) Marital perceptions and interactions across the transition to parenthood. *Journal of Marriage and the Family* 61, 3, 611–25.

Craig, G. J. (1992) *Human Development*, 6th edn. Englewood Cliffs, NJ: Prentice-Hall.

Cramer, D. (1995) Special issue on personal relationships. *The Psychologist* 8, 58–9.

Cuber, J. F. and Harroff, P. B. (1965) *The Significant Americans: A Study of Sexual Behavior among the Affluent*. New York: Appleton-Century-Crofts.

Cummings, E. (1975) Engagement with an old theory. *International Journal of Ageing and Human Development* 6, 187–91.

Cummings, E. and Henry, W. E. (1961) *Growing Old: The Process of Disengagement*. New York: Basic.

Datan, N., Rodeheaver, D. and Hughes, F. (1987) Adult development and ageing. *Annual Review of Psychology*, 38, 153–80.

Denney, N. and Palmer, A. (1981) Adult age differences on traditional problem-solving measures. *Journal of Gerontology* 36, 323–8.

Dergham, H. (2001) http://ccsun7.sogang.ac.kr/~burns/auc-cult/auc-marriageue.html accessed on 14 April 2006.

Dinnerstein, D. (1976) *The Mermaid and the Minotaur: Sexual Arrangements and Human Malaise*. New York: Harper and Row.

Duberman, L. (1973) Step–kin relationships. *Journal of Marriage and the Family* 35, 283–92.

Durkin, K. (1995) *Developmental and Social Psychology: From Infancy to Old Age*. Oxford: Blackwell.

Duval, E. M. (1971) *Family Development*. Philadelphia: J. B. Lippincott.

Erikson, E. H. (1968) *Identity, Youth and Crisis*. New York: W. W. Norton.

Erikson, E. H. (1980) *Identity and the Life Cycle*. New York: Norton.

Eysenck, M. W. (1990) *Psychology: A Student's Handbook*. Hove: Psychology Press.

Galinsky, E. (1981) *Between Generations: The Six Stages of Parenthood*. New York: Berkeley.

Gallagher-Thompson, D. and Thompson, L. W. (2000) in R. C. Clay, Staying in Control, *APA Monitor on Psychology*, 31, 1.

Gilligan, C. (1982) *In a Different Voice: Psychological Theory and Women's Development*. Cambridge, MA: Harvard University Press.

Gottman, J. M. (1998) Psychology and the study of marital processes. *Annual Review of Psychology* 49, 169–97.

Goudge, E. (1940) *The Bird in the Tree*. New York: Popular Library.

Gould, R. L. (1978) *Transformations: Growth and Change in Adult Life*, New York: Simon and Schuster.

Gould, R. L. (1980) Transformational tasks in adulthood. In S. I. Greenspan and G. H. Pollock (eds), *The Course of Life: Psychoanalytic Contributions toward Understanding Personality Development*, Vol. 3: *Adulthood and the Ageing Process*. Washington, DC: National Institute for Mental Health.

Gove, W. R. (1979) The relationship between sex roles, marital status and mental illness. *Social Forces* 51, 34–44.

Gross, R. (2001) *Psychology: The Science of Mind and Behaviour*, 4th edn. London: Hodder and Stoughton.

Gross, R. (1996) *Psychology: The Science of Mind and Behaviour*, 3rd edn. London: Hodder and Stoughton.

Harlow, J. (2001) 'Fledgeling' adults are not grown up until 35. *Sunday Times*, 2 September, 9.

Havighurst, R. J. (1964) Flexibility and the social roles of the retired. *American Journal of Sociology* 59, 309–11.

Havighurst, R. J., Neugarten, B. and Tobin, S. S. (1968) Disengagement and patterns of ageing. In B. L. Neugarten (ed.), *Middle Age and Ageing*. Chicago: University of Chicago Press.

Hetherington, E. M. and Stanley-Hagan, M. (1999) The adjustment of children with divorced parents: A risk and resiliency perspective. *Journal of Child Psychology and Psychiatry* 40 (1), 129–40.

Hodgson, J. W. and Fisher, J. L. (1981) Sex differences in identity and intimacy development in college youth. *Journal of Youth and Adolescence* 8 (1), 37–50.

Holahan, C. K. and Sears, R. R. (1995) *The Gifted Group in Later Maturity*. Stanford, CA: Stanford University Press.

Holmes, T. H. and Rahe, R. H. (1967) The social readjustment rating scale. *Journal of Psychosomatic Research* 11, 213–18.

Horn, J.L. (1982) The ageing of human abilities. In B. Wolman (ed.), *Handbook of Developmental Psychology*. Englewood Cliffs, NJ: Prentice-Hall.

Huxley, A. (1932) *Brave New World*. New York: Doubleday, Doran & Company, Inc.

Jamieson, A. (1990) Home care in old age: A lost cause (Comparative Health Policy). *Journal of Health Politics, Policy & Law* 17, 879–98.

Jones, G. (1995) *Leaving Home*. Buckingham: Open University Press.

Kaffman, M. (1993) Divorce in the kibbutz: Lessons to be drawn. *Family Process* 32 (1), 117–33.

Kamo, Y. (1993) Determinants of marital satisfaction: A comparison of the United States and Japan. *Journal of Social and Personal Relationships* 10 (4), 551–68.

Kastenbaum, R. (1979) Exit and existence: Society's unwritten script for old age and death. In D. D. van Tassel (ed.), *Ageing, Death and the Completion of Being*. Philadelphia: University of Pennsylvania Press.

Keith, P. M. (1977) An exploratory study of sources of stereotypes of old age among administrators. *Journal of Gerontology* 32, 463–9.

Kim, J. E. and Moen, P. (1999) Cited in J. Chamberlin, *Post-retirement Bliss is Different for Men and Women*. APA Monitor, October.

Kline, P. (1992) *Intelligence: The Psychometric View*. London: Routledge.

Levine, R., Sato, S., Hashimoto, T. and Verma, J. (1995) Love and marriage in eleven cultures. *Journal of Cross-Cultural Psychology* 26, 554–71.

Levinson, D.J. (1978) *The Seasons of a Man's Life*. New York: Alfred A. Knopf.

Levinson, D. J. (1986) A conception of adult development. *American Psychologist* 41, 3–13.

Levy, B. and Langer, E. (1994) Aging free from negative stereotypes: Successful memory in China and among the American deaf. *Journal of Personal and Social Psychology* 66, 989–97.

Livson, N. (1981) in C. J. Jones, N. Livson and H. Peskin (2006) *Journal of Research in Personality* 40(1), 56–72.

Loftus, E. F. (1992) When a lie becomes memory's truth: Memory distortion after exposure to misinformation. *Current Directions in Psychological Science*, 1, 121–3.

Lugo, J. O. and Hershey, G. I. (1979) *Lifespan Development*, 2nd edn. London: Macmillan.

McAdams, D. P., de St. Aubin, E. and Logan R. L. (1993) Generativity among young, midlife, and older adults. *Psychology and Aging*, 2, 221–30.

Maslow, A. (1968) *Towards a Psychology of Being*, 2nd edn. New York: Van Nostrand-Reinhold.

Matlin, M. W. (1993) *The Psychology of Women*, 2nd edn. New York: Harcourt, Brace, Jovanovich.

Mead, M. (1949) *Male and Female: A Study of the Sexes in a Changing World*. New York: Dell.

Neugarten, B.L. (1975) Personality and aging. In J. E. Birrin and K. W. Schaie (eds), *Handbook of the Psychology of Aging*. New York: Reinhold.

O'Brien, C. (2001) The art of knowing when to go. *The Times*, 11 September, 2, 8.

Ochse, R. and Plug, C. (1986) Cross-cultural investigation of the validity of Erikson's theory of personality development. *Journal of Personality and Social Psychology* 50, 1240–52.

Parkes, C. M. (1986) *Bereavement: Studies in Grief in Adult life*. London: Tavistock.

Plomin, R. (1997) DNA: Implications. *The Psychologist* 11, 61–2.

Popper, K. R. (1969) *Conjectures and Refutations: The Growth of Scientific Knowledge*. London: Routledge & Kegan Paul.

Presland, P. and Antill, J. K. (1987) Household division of labour: The impact of hours worked in paid employment. *Australian Journal of Psychology* 39(3), 273–91.

Price, W. F. and Crapo, R. H. (1999) *Cross-cultural Perspectives in Introductory Psychology*, 3rd edn. Belmont, CA: Wadsworth Publishing Company.

Rainey, N. (1998) Old age. In K. Trew and J. Kremer (eds), *Gender & Psychology*. London: Arnold.

Ramsay, R.W. and de Groot, W. (1977) A further look at bereavement: Paper presented at EATI conference, Uppsala. Cited in Hodgekinson, P.E. (1980) Treating abnormal grief in the bereaved. *Nursing Times* (17 January), 126–8.

Reibstein, J. and Richards, M. (1992) *Sexual Arrangements: Marriage and Affairs*. London: Heinemann.

Reichard, S., Livson, F. and Peterson, P. G. (1962) *Aging and Personality: A Study of 87 Older Men*. New York: Wiley.

Richardson, S. (2001) cited in J. Harlow, 'Fledgeling' adults are not grown up until 35. *Sunday Times*, 2 September, 9.

Roberts, P. and Newton, P. M. (1987) Levinsonian studies of women's adult development. *Psychology and Aging* 2, 154–63.

Rogers, J., Meyer, J. and Mortel, K. (1990) After reaching retirement age physical activity sustains cerebral perfusion and cognition. *Journal of the American Geriatric Society* 38, 123–8.

Rotter, J. B. (1966) Generalised expectancies for internal vs external control of reinforcement. *Psychological Monographs* 80 (1).

Ruble, D. N., Fleming, A. S., Hackel, L. S. and Stangor, C. (1988) Changes in the marital relationship during the transition to first time motherhood: The effects of violated expectations concerning division of household labour. *Journal of Personality and Social Psychology* 55, 78–87.

Rutter, M. and Rutter, M. (1992) *Developing Minds: Challenge and Continuity across the Life-Span*. Harmondsworth: Penguin.

Sangiuliano, I. (1978) *In Her Time*. New York: Morrow.

Schaie, K. W. and Hetzog, C. (1983) Fourteen-year cohort-sequential analysis of adult intellectual development. *Developmental Psychology* 19, 531–43.

Schumm, W. R., Webb, F. J. and Bullman, S. R. (1998) Gender and marital satisfaction: Data from a national survey of families and households. *Psychological Reports* 83 (1), 319–27.

Schwarzer, R. and Leppin, A. (1992) Social support and mental health: A conceptual and empirical overview. In L. Montada, S. H. Filipp and M. J. Lerner (eds), *Life Crises and Experiences of Loss in Adulthood*. Hillsdale, NJ: Lawrence Erlbaum.

Sheehy, G. (1996) *New Passages*. New York: HarperCollins.

Social Trends (1999) Office for National Statistics (Great Britain) *Social Trends 29*, ed. J. Matheson and J. Pullinger. London: The Stationery Office.

Streib, G. F. and Schneider, C. J. (1971) *Retirement in American Society: Impact and Process*. Ithaca, NY: Cornell University Press.

Stroebe, M. S., Stroebe, W. and Hansson, R. O. (1993) Contemporary themes and controversies in bereavement research. In M. S. Stroebe, W. Stroebe and R. O. Hansson (eds), *Handbook of Bereavement: Theory, Research and Intervention*. New York: Cambridge University Press.

Sugarman, L. (1986) *Lifespan Development: Concepts, Theories and Interventions*. London: Methuen.

Swenson, C. H., Eskew, R. W. and Kolheff, K. A. (1981) Stages of family life cycle, ego development and the marriage relationship. *Journal of Marriage and the Family* 43, 842–53.

Taylor, S. E., Klein, L. C., Lewis, B. P., Gruenewald, T. L., Gurung, R. A. R. and Updegraff, J. A. (2000) Biobehavioural responses to stress in females: Tend-and-befriend, not fight-or-flight. *Psychological Review* 107, 411–29.

Thoits, P. A. (1982) Direct, indirect and moderating effects of social support on psychological distress and associated conditions. In H. B. Kaplan (ed.), *Psychosocial Stress: Trends in Theory and Research*. New York: Academic Press.

Tout, K. (1989) *Ageing in Developing Countries*. Oxford: Oxford University Press

Turnbull, C. M. (1989) *The Mountain People*. London: Paladin.

Turnbull, S. K. (1995) The middle years. In D. Wedding (ed.), *Behaviour and Medicine*, 2nd edn. St Louis, MO: Mosby Year Book.

Turner, J. S. and Helms, D. B. (1989) *Contemporary Adulthood*, 4th edn. Fort Worth, FL: Holt, Rinehart & Winston.

Valliant, G.E. (1977) *Adaptation to Life*. Boston, MA: Little, Brown.

Valliant, C. O. and Valliant, G. E. (1993) Is the U-curve of marital satisfaction an illusion? A 40-year study of marriage. *Journal of Marriage and the Family* 55, 230–9.

Veroff, J. and Feld, S. (1970) *Marriage and Work in America: A Study of Motives and Roles*. New York: Van Nostrand Reinhold.

Walker, K. (1970) cited in D. V. Heller, Power dependence and division of family work (1984). *Sex Roles* 10 (11–12), 1003–19.

Wechsler, D. (1958) *The Measurement and Appraisal of Adult Intelligence*, 4th edn. Baltimore: Williams and Wilkins.

Whitbourne, S. K. and Weinstock, C. S. (1979) *Adult Development: The Differentiation of Experience*. New York: Holt, Rinehart and Winston.

Wright, E. O., Shire, K., Hwang, S-L., Dolan, M. and Baxter, J. (1992) The non-effects of class on the gender division of labor in the home: A comparative study of Sweden and the United States. *Gender and Society* 6, 2 , 252–82.

Index